EASY
SPANISH
PHRASE
BOOK

NEW EDITION

Over 700 Phrases
for Everyday Use

Pablo García Loaeza, Ph.D.

DOVER PUBLICATIONS, INC.
Mineola, New York

Copyright

Bibliographical Note

Easy Spanish Phrase Book NEW EDITION: Over 700 Phrases for Everyday Use, first published by Dover Publications, Inc., in 2013, is a new selection of material from *1001 Easy Spanish Phrases*, published in 2010 by Dover Publications, Inc.

Library of Congress Cataloging-in-Publication Data

Loaeza, Pablo García, 1972–
    Easy Spanish phrase book : over 700 phrases for everyday use / Pablo García Loaeza. — New ed.
        p. cm. —
    "First published by Dover Publications, Inc., in 2013, is a new selection of material from 1001 Easy Spanish Phrases, published in 2010 by Dover Publications, Inc."
    Includes index.
    ISBN-13: 978-0-486-49905-5 — ISBN-10: 0-486-49905-7
        1. Spanish language—Conversation and phrase books—English.
    2. Spanish language—Spoken Spanish. I. Title. II. Title: 1001 easy
Spanish phrases.
    PC4121.L55 2013
    468.3'421—dc23

                                                        2012021714

Manufactured in the United States by LSC Communications
49905705   2017
www.doverpublications.com

Contents

Introduction

This book will let you become familiar with a basic set of sentences, phrases, and words for simple everyday communication in Spanish. In particular, the would-be visitor to a Spanish-speaking country will find the tools necessary to deal with common situations related to travel abroad. The different sections cover topics such as transportation, accommodation, eating and drinking, as well as sightseeing, and shopping. There are also sections that cover a number of problems that may arise. Each section takes account of dialectic variation in Spanish by pointing out when a specific word is used in Spain (Sp.) or a particular Latin American country (Mex., Arg., etc.). When appropriate, entries indicate whether the corresponding Spanish sentence is formal (for.) or informal (inf.).

The book was designed to serve as a useful foundation rather than an exhaustive field manual. It is meant to be used for reference, study, and review. The more you practice the essential structures included here, the easier it will be for you to generate the questions and statements appropriate to your specific needs and circumstances. When you are communicating with someone, the other person is also trying to make sense of what you are saying and drawing information not just from your words, but also from context, tone of voice, and body language. When you need an answer, looking a person in the eye is generally more practical and more effective than reading from a book.

To facilitate acquisition, the material included in the different sections is presented in a logical sequence. As you go through the sentences, imagine yourself in the situations they suggest. In the "Eating & Drinking" section, for instance, you can go from finding a restaurant to asking for the check after ordering breakfast, lunch or dinner, and dessert. Since the material is not cumulative, book sections can be studied according to need or preference. You will note that certain structures, such as "I want . . ." and "where is . . . ," appear frequently throughout the book. Besides being very handy, their repetition facilitates focusing on the many complementary words and phrases. Thus, you can learn to produce a large number of sentences and convey a wide range of information with minimum effort.

Finally, while practice trumps theory, the Spanish Grammar Primer included here will help you make the most of the book. Besides vocabulary-building tips and verb conjugation tables, it contains information about nouns, adjectives, pronouns, and prepositions. However, many people will find Dover's *Essential Spanish Grammar* (ISBN 0-486-20780-3) helpful for mastering the subtleties of the Spanish language. Likewise, *2,001 Most Useful Spanish Words* (ISBN 0-486-47616-2), also published by Dover, is a useful complement for increasing your Spanish vocabulary further.

A Note on Spanish Dialects

As with English, there are many regional dialects of Spanish. They may vary in pronunciation, vocabulary, and syntax but they are all mutually intelligible.

For instance, in the Castile region of Spain a "c" before an "e" or an "i" sounds like "th" in English and the letter "s" is pronounced like "sh." On the other hand, people in the south of Spain and in Latin America, generally make the letter "c" (before "e" or "i"), the letter "s," and even the letter "z" all sound like the "s" in "soup." Caribbean Spanish tends to drop a "d" between two vowels at the end of some words, as well as a final "s" so that *cansados* (tired, m. pl.) becomes *cansao*. Likewise, in many South American countries the word for cake is *torta*, whereas in Mexico it is *pastel*. In Latin America a computer is called *una computadora* while in Spain it is referred to as *un ordenador*. Nevertheless, a Spaniard, a Mexican, a Chilean, and a Dominican can engage in conversation without impediment.

When Spanish is learned as a second language the choice of dialect can depend on personal interest and circumstance. For example, someone traveling to Spain might prefer to become familiar with the Castilian dialect, while someone spending time in a Latin American country will pick up the local accent and lingo. The best investment for a beginner studying stateside is to practice a "neutral" kind of Spanish: all the syllables in a word should be pronounced clearly, using the standard word-stress rules (see the grammar section). Once you know the basic system, a little practice makes it easy to compensate for dialectical differences. Remember also that the most useful words, such as *por favor* and *gracias*, are the same throughout the Spanish-speaking world.

Unlike English—-in which the same word may be written one way in Britain (colour, dialogue, emphasise, gaol) and another in the United States (color, dialog, emphasize, jail), all Spanish dialects use the same written standard.

Phonetic Transcription

The phonetic transcription of the Spanish words and phrases is provided as an aid to an approximately correct pronunciation in the absence of an audio model. However, the Spanish sound scheme is very regular and straightforward; with some practice you should be able to bypass the phonetic transcription in most instances.

Other than the International Phonetic Alphabet, which employs a special set of characters, there is no standard for phonetic transcription. In order to facilitate reading, the phonetic transcription in this book follows the rules of English pronunciation and spelling as closely as possible. For instance, vowels are short before a double consonant (as in "dress"); the letter "c" is hard before an "a" or an "o" (as in "car"), but soft before an "e" (as in "celery"); etc. The syllables that should be stressed are underlined.

The phonetic transcription presented here corresponds to a "neutral" dialect of Spanish which, pronounced correctly, will be understood in any Spanish-speaking country.

Phonetic transcription key:

ah	A as in father and drama.
ay	long A as in stay, weigh, and train.
ch	as in chat, chess, and cheese.
ee	long E as in feet and eel.
eh, ess	short E as in pet, let, less, and rest.
ehr	sounds like air.
g	hard G as in gap, get, and geese.[1]
h	H as in ham, heel, and hot.
I, i	long I as in the first person pronoun.
k	hard C as in cat, cot, and cool, or K as in king.

---

[1] In Spanish an intervocalic G tends towards vocalization and will be represented by a "w" in order to reflect actual pronunciation better. For example, *agua* (water) will be transcripted as "<u>ah</u>-wah."

ny	as in barnyard and canyon.
oh	long O as in hope, open, and cone.
oo	OO as in moon and soon.
oy	as in boy, soy, and toy.
s	as in sat, set, or soft C as in cellar and central.
w	as in well and wet.
y	as in yard and yet.

Spanish Pronunciation

Vowels

Spanish only has five vowel sounds (English has over 15!) which correspond to the five vowel letters, regardless of their position in a word. There are no silent vowels in Spanish. The five vowel sounds in Spanish are:

a as in drama	*Habla a la casa blanca.*	Call the White House.
e as in bet	*Él es el rebelde René Pérez.*	He is the rebel René Pérez.
i as in deep	*Sí, viví sin ti.*	Yes, I lived without you.
o as in coat	*Los locos no son tontos.*	Crazy people aren't dumb.
u as in loop	*Fui a un club nocturno.*	I went to a nightclub.

The semi-consonant y is pronounced like i [ee] when used as a conjunction: Pedro y María (*Pedro and María*); its sound softens next to a vowel (as in yellow): Juan y yo somos muy buenos amigos (*Juan and I are very good friends*).

Consonants

Spanish has basically the same consonant sounds as English. However, there are a few particulars to keep in mind:

b and v are very often pronounced the same way, as in "bee."

c (soft), s, and z vary in pronunciation in some Spanish dialects. However, in all but the rarest cases, they can all be pronounced like the s in "soft" without risk of confusion.

g is hard as in good before a, o, and u, but soft as in horse before e or i.

gu is used before e and i to represent a hard g sound as in good (note that here the **u** does not function as a vowel; **gu** is a digraph in which two letters represent a single sound as in **th**e).

h is always mute as in **h**erbs.

j is pronounced like the **h** in **h**orse.

ll is always pronounced as the **y** in **y**ellow.

ñ represents a particular sound which resembles the **ny** combination found in ca**ny**on.

qu is used before **e** and **i** to represent a hard **c** sound as in **c**at (see **gu** above).

r at the beginning of a word is trilled.

rr represents a trill in the middle of a word.

Stress and written accents

Spanish words tend to have two or more syllables; when they are pronounced one syllable always sounds a little bit louder than the others. The stressed syllable is either the last, the penultimate (most often), or the antepenultimate syllable (least often). Word stress in Spanish is determined by two simple rules:

1. Words that end in a **vowel**, **n**, or **s** are generally pronounced stressing the **next to last syllable**:
   Ven*ta*na (*window*), *bar*co (*boat*), pa*lab*ras (*words*), tú *can*tas (*you sing*), ellos *com*en (*they eat*)
2. Words which end in a **consonant** other than **n** or **s** are generally stressed on the **last syllable**:
   pa*pel* (*paper*), fe*liz* (*happy*), acti*tud* (*attitude*), can*tar* (*to sing*), com*er* (*to eat*)

Written accent marks are used when a word's pronunciation is at odds with these rules. In other words, accent marks indicate a stress where you wouldn't normally expect it.

Thus, words which end in a vowel, **n**, or **s** but require the stress to fall on the last syllable need a written accent mark to "drag" the sound forward:

ciem*piés* (*centipede*), can*ción* (*song*), él can*tó* (*he sang*),[2] yo co*mí* (*I ate*)

---

[2] Note the difference with yo *can*to (*I sing*): a change in stress can significantly change the meaning of a word or even a whole sentence.

Conversely, words that need the stress to fall on the next to last syllable but end in a consonant other than **n** or **s** need a written accent mark to "drag" the sound backward:

lápiz (*pencil*), árbol (*tree*), azúcar (*sugar*), carácter (*character*)

Finally, words that need the stress on the antepenultimate syllable always have a written accent:

murciélago (*bat*)[3], círculo (*circle*), lágrima (*eye tear*), cántalo (*sing it*)

---

[3] Repeating the word **murciélago** out loud is a good way to practice pronunciation: it has all five vowel sounds and distinctive stress.

NUMBERS

zero	*cero*	<u>seh</u>-roh
one	*uno*	<u>oo</u>-noh
two	*dos*	dohss
three	*tres*	trehss
four	*cuatro*	<u>kwah</u>-troh
five	*cinco*	<u>seen</u>-koh
six	*seis*	<u>sayss</u>
seven	*siete*	see-<u>eh</u>-teh
eight	*ocho*	<u>oh</u>-choh
nine	*nueve*	<u>nweh</u>-veh
ten	*diez*	dee-<u>ess</u>
eleven	*once*	<u>ohn</u>-seh
twelve	*doce*	<u>doh</u>-seh
thirteen	*trece*	<u>treh</u>-seh
fourteen	*catorce*	kah-<u>tor</u>-seh
fifteen	*quince*	<u>keen</u>-seh
sixteen	*dieciséis*	dee-eh-see-<u>sayss</u>
seventeen	*diecisiete*	dee-eh-see-see-<u>eh</u>-teh
eighteen	*dieciocho*	dee-eh-see-<u>oh</u>-choh
nineteen	*diecinueve*	dee-eh-see-<u>nweh</u>-veh
twenty	*veinte*	<u>vayn</u>-teh
twenty-one	*veintiuno*	vayn-tee-<u>oo</u>-noh
twenty-two	*veintidós*	vayn-tee-<u>dohss</u>
thirty	*treinta*	<u>trayn</u>-tah
thirty-one	*treinta y uno*	<u>trayn</u>-tah ee <u>oo</u>-noh
thirty-two	*treinta y dos*	<u>trayn</u>-tah ee dohss
forty	*cuarenta*	kwah-<u>ren</u>-tah

fifty	*cincuenta*	seen-<u>kwen</u>-tah
sixty	*sesenta*	seh-<u>sen</u>-tah
seventy	*setenta*	seh-<u>ten</u>-tah
eighty	*ochenta*	oh-<u>chen</u>-tah
ninety	*noventa*	noh-<u>ven</u>-tah
one hundred	*cien*	see-<u>en</u>
one hundred and one	*ciento uno*	see-<u>en</u>-toh <u>oo</u>-noh
one hundred and two	*ciento dos*	see-<u>en</u>-toh dohss
two hundred	*doscientos*	dohss-see-<u>en</u>-tohss
three hundred	*trescientos*	trehss-see-<u>en</u>-tohss
four hundred	*cuatrocientos*	kwah-troh-see-<u>en</u>-tohss
five hundred	*quinientos*	kee-nee-<u>en</u>-tohss
six hundred	*seiscientos*	sayss-see-<u>en</u>-tohss
seven hundred	*setecientos*	seh-teh-see-<u>en</u>-tohss
eight hundred	*ochocientos*	oh-choh-see-<u>en</u>-tohss
nine hundred	*novecientos*	noh-veh-see-<u>en</u>-tohss
one thousand	*mil*	meel
two thousand	*dos mil*	dohss-<u>meel</u>
one hundred thousand	*cien mil*	see-<u>en</u> meel
million	*millón*	mee-<u>yohn</u>
two million	*dos millones*	dohss mee-<u>yoh</u>-ness

1. I need to add up these numbers.
   Necesito sumar estos números.
   Neh-seh-<u>see</u>-toh soo-<u>mar</u> ess-tohss <u>noo</u>-meh-rohss

2. How much is one plus one?   *¿Cuánto es uno más uno?*
   <u>Kwahn</u>-toh ess <u>oo</u>-noh mahss <u>oo</u>-noh

3. What's the total?   *¿Cuál es el total?*   Kwahl ess el toh-<u>tahl</u>

COLORS

4. What's your favorite color?   *¿Cuál es tu color favorito?*
   Kwahl ess too koh-<u>lor</u> fah-voh-<u>ree</u>-toh

5. My favorite color is blue.   *Mi color favorito es azul.*
   Mee koh-<u>lor</u> fah-voh-<u>ree</u>-toh ess ah-<u>sool</u>

black.	*negro.*	**neh-groh**
brown.	*café/marrón.*	**kah-<u>feh</u>/mah-<u>ron</u>**
green.	*verde.*	**<u>vehr</u>-deh**
gray.	*gris.*	**greess**
orange.	*anaranjado.*	**ah-nah-rahn-<u>hah</u>-doh**
pink.	*rosa.*	**<u>roh</u>-sah**
purple.	*morado.*	**moh-<u>rah</u>-doh**
red.	*rojo.*	**<u>roh</u>-hoh**
white.	*blanco.*	**<u>blahn</u>-koh**
yellow.	*amarillo.*	**ah-mah-<u>ree</u>-yoh**

MEETING & GREETING

6. Hello.   *Hola.*   **<u>Oh</u>-lah**

7. Good morning/day.   *Buenos días.*   **<u>Bweh</u>-nohss <u>dee</u>-ahss**

8. Good afternoon.   *Buenas tardes.*   **<u>Bweh</u>-nahss <u>tar</u>-dess**

9. Good evening/night.   *Buenas noches.*
   <u>Bweh</u>-nahss <u>noh</u>-chess

10. Welcome.   *Bienvenido/-a(s).*   **Bee-en-veh-<u>nee</u>-doh/-ah(ss)**

11. Come in.   *Adelante./Pase(n).*   **Ah-dehl-<u>ahn</u>-teh/<u>Pah</u>-seh(n)**

12. Pleased to meet you.   *Es un placer (-conocerlo/-a).*
    Ess oon plah-<u>sehr</u> (-koh-noh-<u>sehr</u>-loh/-ah)

13. Nice to meet you.   *Mucho gusto (en conocerlo/-a).*
    <u>Moo</u>-choh <u>goos</u>-toh (en koh-noh-<u>sehr</u>-loh/-ah)

14. The pleasure is mine.   *El gusto es mío.*
El **goos**-toh ess **mee**-oh

15. What's your name? (for.)   *¿Cómo se llama (usted)?*
Koh-moh seh **yah**-mah (oos-**ted**)
What's your name? (inf.)   *. . . te llamas?*   teh **yah**-mahss

16. I'm called . . .   *Me llamo . . .*   Meh **yah**-moh

17. My name is . . .   *Mi nombre es . . .*   Mee **nohm**-breh ess . . .

18. Where are you from? (for./inf.)   *¿De dónde es/eres?*
Deh **dohn**-deh ess/ **eh**-ress

19. I'm from . . .   *Soy de . . .*   Soy deh

20. Let me introduce you to . . . (for./inf.)
Le/te presento a . . .   Leh/teh preh-**sen**-toh ah

21. How are you? (for./inf.)   *¿Cómo está(s)?*
Koh-moh ess-**tahss**

22. How's it going? (for./inf.)   *¿Cómo le/te va?*
Koh-moh leh/teh vah

23. Very well/Fine, thank you.   *(Muy) Bien, gracias.*
(Mooy) Bee-**en**, **grah**-see-ahss

24. So-so.   *Más o menos./Así así. (Sp.)*
Mahss oh **meh**-nohss/Ah-**see** ah-**see**

25. (Very) bad.   *(Muy) Mal.*   (Mooy) Mahl

26. And yourself? (for./inf.)   *¿Y usted/tú?*   Ee oos-**ted**/too

27. What's new?   *¿Qué hay de nuevo?*   Keh I deh **nweh**-voh

28. I don't know.   *No sé.*   Noh seh

29. Nothing.   *Nada.*   **Nah**-dah

30. Good-bye.   *Adiós.*   Ah-dee-**ohss**

31. See you later.   *Nos vemos./Hasta luego.*
Nohss **veh**-mohss/-**Ahss**-tah **lweh**-goh

32. See you soon. *Hasta pronto.* **Ahss**-tah **prohn**-toh

33. See you tomorrow. *Hasta mañana.*
    Ahss-tah mah-**nyah**-nah

34. Until we meet again. *Hasta la vista/la próxima.*
    Ahss-tah lah **vees**-tah/lah **prohk**-see-mah

35. When will we meet again? *¿Cuándo nos volveremos a ver?*
    Kwahn-doh nohss vohl-veh-**reh**-mohss ah vehr

36. Hopefully it won't be long. *Ojalá no pase mucho tiempo.*
    Oh-hah-**lah** noh **pah**-seh **moo**-choh tee-**em**-poh

37. Have a nice day. *Que te vaya bien.*
    Keh teh **vah**-yah bee-**en**

38. I hope you had a good time. *Espero que se hayan divertido.*
    Ess-**peh**-roh keh seh **I**-ahn dee-vehr-**tee**-doh

39. I had a (very) good time. *La pasé (muy) bien.*
    Lah pah-**seh** (mooy) bee-**en**

40. Come back soon! *¡Regresen pronto!*
    Reh-**greh**-sen-**prohn**-toh

41. Good luck. *(Buena) Suerte.* (-**Bweh**-nah) **Swehr**-teh

42. Take care. *Cuídate.* -**Kwee**-**dah**-teh

BASIC COURTESY

43. Please. *Por favor.* Por fah-**vor**

44. Thank you (very much). *(Muchas) Gracias.*
    (**Moo**-chahss) **Grah**-see-ahss

45. Thanks for everything. *Gracias por todo.*
    Grah-see-ahss por **toh**-doh

46. You're welcome. *De nada./No hay de qué.*
    Deh **nah**-dah/Noh I deh keh

47. Excuse me. (for.)   *Disculpe./Perdóneme.*
    Dees-kool-peh/Pehr-doh-neh-meh

48. I wouldn't want to bother you. (for.)   *No quisiera molestarlo.*
    Noh kee-see-eh-rah moh-less-tar-loh

49. I hope it's not too much of a bother.
    Espero que no sea mucha molestia.
    Ess-peh-roh keh noh seh-ah moo-chah moh-less-tee-ah

50. If you don't mind.   *Si no le importa.*
    See noh leh eem-por-tah

51. I would like to . . .   *Me gustaría . . .*   **Meh goos-tah-ree-ah**

52. May I . . . ?   *¿Puedo . . . ?*   **Pweh-doh**

53. Sure, absolutely.   *¿Cómo no?*   **Koh-moh noh**

54. It's ok.   *Está bien.*   **Ess-tah bee-en**

55. No problem.   *No hay problema.*   **Noh I proh-bleh-mah**

56. Of course.   *No faltaba más.*   **Noh fahl-tah-bah mahss**

57. Allow me. (for.)   *Permítame.*   **Pehr-mee-tah-meh**

58. Gladly.   *Con gusto.*   **Kohn goos-toh**

59. Don't bother. (for.)   *No se moleste.*   **Noh seh moh-less-teh**

60. Don't worry. (for.)   *No se preocupe.*
    Noh seh preh-oh-koo-peh

61. I'm sorry.   *Lo siento.*   **Loh see-en-toh**

62. Bless you.   *Salud.*   **Sah-lood**

HOW DO YOU SAY . . . ?

63. Do you speak English? (for./inf.)   *¿Habla(s) inglés?*
    Ah-blah(s) een-gless

64. Does anyone here speak English?   *¿Alguien aquí habla inglés?*
    Ahl-gee-en ah-kee ah-blah een-gless

65. Do you understand me? (for./inf.)   *¿Me entiende(s)?*
    Meh en-tee-<u>en</u>-deh(ss)

66. I don't understand.   *No entiendo/comprendo.*
    Noh en-tee-<u>en</u>-doh/kohm-<u>pren</u>-doh

67. I'm confused.   *Estoy confundido.*
    Ess-<u>toy</u> kohn-foon-<u>dee</u>-doh

68. I don't speak Spanish.   *No hablo español.*
    Noh <u>ah</u>-bloh ess-pah-<u>nyohl</u>

69. I speak a little Spanish.   *Hablo un poco de español.*
    <u>Ah</u>-bloh oon <u>poh</u>-koh deh ess-pah-<u>nyohl</u>

70. I don't know this word.   *No conozco esta palabra.*
    Noh koh-<u>nohss</u>-koh <u>ess</u>-tah pah-<u>lah</u>-brah

71. I didn't hear you correctly. (for.)   *No lo escuché bien.*
    Noh loh ess-koo-<u>cheh</u> bee-<u>en</u>

72. Say again, please. (for.)   *Repita, por favor.*
    Reh-<u>pee</u>-tah, por fah-<u>vor</u>

73. Not so fast.   *No tan rápido.*   **Noh tahn <u>rah</u>-pee-doh.**

74. Speak slower, please. (for.)   *Hable más despacio, por favor.*
    <u>Ah</u>-bleh mahss dess-<u>pah</u>-see-oh, por fah-<u>vor</u>

75. What does . . . mean?   *¿Qué significa . . . ?*
    Keh seeg-nee-<u>fee</u>-kah

76. What does this say?   *¿Qué dice aquí?*   **Keh <u>dee</u>-seh ah-<u>kee</u>**

77. How do you say . . . in Spanish?
    ¿Cómo se dice . . . en español?
    <u>Koh</u>-moh seh <u>dee</u>-seh . . . en ess-pah-<u>nyohl</u>

78. How do you pronounce this word?
    ¿Cómo se pronuncia esta palabra?
    <u>Koh</u>-moh seh proh-<u>noon</u>-see-ah <u>ess</u>-tah pah-<u>lah</u>-brah

79. Can you translate it for me? (for./inf.)
    ¿Me lo puede(s) traducir?
    Meh loh <u>pweh</u>-deh(dess) trah-doo-<u>seer</u>

80. Can you write it down? (for./inf.)   *¿Puede(s) escribirlo?*
Pweh-deh(dess) es-kree-**beer**-loh

81. How do you spell it?   *¿Cómo se deletrea?*
Koh-moh seh deh-leh-**treh**-ah

82. Do you have a dictionary? (for./inf.)
¿Tiene(s) un diccionario?
Tee-**eh**-neh (nehss) oon deek-see-oh-**nah**-ree-oh

THE BASICS

83. I have a problem.   *Tengo un problema.*
Ten-goh oon proh-**bleh**-mah

84. I am lost. (m./f.)   *Estoy perdido/a.*   Ess-**toy** pehr-**dee**-doh/ah

85. I don't know where I am.   *No sé dónde estoy.*
Noh seh **dohn**-deh ess-**toy**

86. Help me, please. (for.)   *Ayúdeme, por favor.*
Ah-**yoo**-deh-meh, por fah-**vor**

87. Can you help me? (for./inf.)   *¿Me puede(s) ayudar?*
Meh **pweh**-deh(s) ah-yoo-**dar**

88. Who can I ask?   *¿A quién le puedo preguntar?*
Ah kee-**en** leh **pweh**-doh preh-goon-**tar**

89. I need help.   *Necesito ayuda.*   Neh-seh-**see**-toh ah-**yoo**-dah
information.   *información.*   een-for-mah-see-**ohn**
a city map.   *un mapa de la ciudad.*
oon **mah**-pah deh lah **see**-oo-dahd
money.   *dinero.*   dee-**neh**-roh
food.   *comida.*   koh-**mee**-dah

90. I'm looking for something to eat/drink.
Estoy buscando algo de comer/beber.
Ess-**toy** boos-**kahn**-doh **ahl**-goh deh koh-**mehr**/beh-**behr**

91. Where is there a restroom?
¿Dónde hay un baño/ unos servicios? (Sp.)
Dohn-deh I oon **bah**-nyoh/**oo**-nohss sehr-**vee**-see-ohss

92. Can I make a phone call?
¿Puedo hacer una llamada (telefónica)?
Pweh-doh ah-**sehr** **oo**-nah yah-**mah**-dah (teh-leh-**foh**-nee-kah)

93. I need to go to the (U.S.) consulate/the embassy.
Necesito ir al consulado/a la embajada (de Estados Unidos).
Neh-seh-**see**-toh eer ahl kohn-sool-**ah**-doh/ah lah
em-bah-**hah**-dah deh Ess-**tah**-dohss Oo-**nee**-dohss

94. Can I use the phone?   *¿Puedo usar el teléfono?*
Pweh-doh oo-**sar** el teh-**leh**-foh-noh

the restroom?   *el baño/los servicios? (Sp.)*
cl **bah**-nyoh/lohss sehr **vee**-see-ohss

95. It's urgent.   *Es urgente.*   Ess oor-**hen**-teh

96. Where is the train station?
¿Dónde está la estación de tren?
Dohn-deh ess-**tah** lah ess-tah-see-**ohn** deh tren

police station?   *de policía?*   deh poh-lee-**see**-ah
bus station?   *de autobús?*   deh ow-toh-**boos**

97. Please take me to the airport.
Por favor lléveme al aeropuerto.
Por fah-**vor** **yeh**-veh-meh ah ahl I-roh-**pwehr**-toh

98. I want to go back home.   *Quiero regresar a casa.*
Kee-**eh**-roh reh-greh-**sar** ah **kah**-sah

to the hotel.   *al hotel.*   ahl oh-**tel**

99. Where can I find a drugstore?
¿Dónde puedo encontrar una farmacia?
Dohn-deh **pweh**-doh en-kohn-**trar** **oo**-nah far-**mah**-see-ah

a supermarket?   *un supermercado?*
oon **soo**-pehr mehr-**kah**-doh

a travel agency?   *una agencia de viajes?*
oo-nah ah-**hen**-see-ah deh vee-**ah**-hess

100. What is this/that?   *¿Qué es esto/eso?*
Keh ess **ess**-toh/-**eh**-soh

101. Who is he/she?   *¿Quién es él/ella?*   Kee-**en** ess el/-**eh**-yah

102. When do we eat?   *¿Cuándo comemos?*
      <u>Kwahn</u>-doh koh-<u>meh</u>-mohss

103. Where are we?   *¿Dónde estamos?*
      <u>Dohn</u>-deh ess-<u>tah</u>-mohss

104. Where are we going?   *¿A dónde vamos?*
      Ah <u>dohn</u>-deh <u>vah</u>-mohss

105. How can we get to . . . ?   *¿Cómo podemos llegar a . . . ?*
      <u>Koh</u>-moh poh-<u>deh</u>-mohss yeh-<u>gar</u> ah

106. What for?   *¿Para qué?*   <u>Pah</u>-rah keh

107. Why (not)?   *¿Por qué (no)?*   Por keh (noh)

108. I won't.   *No quiero.*   Noh kee-<u>eh</u>-roh

109. I can't.   *No puedo.*   Noh <u>pweh</u>-doh

PERSONAL PORTRAITS & EMOTIONS

110. Can you describe the person?
      ¿Puede describir a la persona?
      <u>Pweh</u>-deh dess-kree-<u>beer</u> ah lah pehr-<u>soh</u>-nah

111. What does he/she look like?   *¿Cómo es?*   <u>Koh</u>-moh ess

112. How old is he/she?   *¿Cuántos años tiene?*
      <u>Kwahn</u>-tohss <u>ah</u>-nyohss tee-<u>eh</u>-neh

113. He/she is young/old.   *Es joven/viejo.*
      Ess <u>hoh</u>-vehn/vee-<u>eh</u>-hoh

114. He/she is a child.
      Es un niño/a.
      Ess oon <u>nee</u>-nyoh/ah

115. What's his/her weight?   *¿Cuánto pesa?*
      <u>Kwahn</u>-toh <u>peh</u>-sah

116. He/she weighs around 180/130 pounds.
      Pesa más o menos ochenta/sesenta kilos.
      <u>Peh</u>-sah mahss oh <u>meh</u>-nohss oh-<u>chen</u>-tah/ seh-<u>sen</u>-tah
      <u>kee</u>-lohss

117. What is his/her height?   *¿Cuánto mide?*
Kwahn-toh **mee**-deh

118. He/she is 6/5 feet tall.   *Mide un metro ochenta/cincuenta.*
Mee-deh oon **meh**-troh oh-**chen**-tah/seen-**kwen**-tah

119. What does he/she look like?   *¿Cómo es?*   **Koh**-moh ess

120. He/she has short/long hair.   *Tiene el pelo corto/largo.*
Tee-**eh**-neh el **peh**-loh **kor**-toh/**lar**-goh

    straight/curly.   *lacio/rizado.*   **lah**-see-oh/ree-**sah**-doh

    light/dark.   *claro/oscuro.*   **klah**-roh/ohss-**koo**-roh

121. He/she is bald.   *Es calvo/a.*   Ess **cahl**-voh/ah

122. He/she has fair/dark skin.   *Tiene la piel clara/oscura.*
Tee-**eh**-neh lah pee-**el** **klah**-rah/ohss-**koo**-rah

    pale.   *pálida.*   **pah**-lee-dah

123. He/she has light/dark colored eyes.
Tiene los ojos claros/oscuros.
Tee-**eh**-neh lohss **oh**-hohss **klah**-rohss/ohss-**koo**-rohss

124. He wears a moustache/beard.
Lleva bigote/barba.
Yeh-vah bee-**goh**-teh/**bar**-bah

125. He/she is (very) fat.   *Es (muy) gordo/a.*
Ess (mooy) **gor**-doh/ah

    thin. (m./f.)   *flaco/a.*   **flah**-koh/ah

    short. (m./f.)   *bajo/a.*   **bah**-hoh/ah

    tall. (m./f.)   *alto/a.*   **ahl**-toh/ah

126. He/she has a tattoo.   *Tiene un tatuaje.*
Tee-**eh**-neh oon tah-**twah**-heh

127. He/she has a piercing.
Tiene un pirsin.
Tee-**eh**-neh oon **peer**-seen

128. He is very ugly/handsome.   *Es muy feo/guapo.*
Ess (mooy) **feh**-oh/**gwah**-poh

129. She is very ugly/beautiful.   *Es muy fea/bella.*
Ess (mooy) **feh**-ah/**beh**-yah

130. He/she is a (very) happy/serious person.
Es una persona (muy) alegre/seria.
Ess <u>oo</u>-nah pehr-<u>soh</u>-nah (mooy) ah-<u>leh</u>-greh/<u>seh</u>-ree-ah

131. He/she is a (very) funny person.
Es una persona (muy) chistosa.
Ess <u>oo</u>-nah pehr-<u>soh</u>-nah (mooy) chees-<u>toh</u>-sah

132. He/she is a (very) intelligent person.
Es una persona (muy) inteligente.
Ess <u>oo</u>-nah pehr-<u>soh</u>-nah (mooy) een-teh-lee-<u>hen</u>-teh

133. He's a great guy.   *Es un gran tipo.*   **Ess oon grahn <u>tee</u>-poh**

134. I like him/her (a lot).   *Me cae (muy) bien.*
Meh <u>kah</u>-eh (mooy) bee-<u>en</u>

135. I dislike him/her (a lot).   *Me cae (muy) mal.*
Meh <u>kah</u>-eh (mooy) mahl

136. I can't stand him/her.   *No lo/la soporto.*
Noh loh/lah soh-<u>por</u>-toh

137. I detest him/her.   *Lo/la detesto.*   **Loh/lah deh-<u>tess</u>-toh**

138. I hate him/her.   *Lo/la odio.*   **Loh/lah <u>oh</u>-dee-oh**

139. He/she seems (very) happy/depressed.
Se le ve (muy) feliz/deprimido.
Seh leh veh (mooy) feh-<u>lees</u>/deh-pree-<u>mee</u>-doh

140. I feel (very) happy/sad.   *Me siento (muy) feliz/triste.*
Meh see-<u>en</u>-toh (mooy) feh-<u>lees</u>/<u>trees</u>-teh

141. I feel like crying.   *Tengo ganas de llorar.*
<u>Ten</u>-goh <u>gah</u>-nahss deh yoh-<u>rar</u>

142. I'm (very) angry.   *Estoy (muy) enojado.*
Ess-<u>toy</u> (mooy) eh-noh-<u>hah</u>-doh

143. I'm (very) scared.   *Tengo (mucho) miedo.*
<u>Ten</u>-goh (-<u>moo</u>-choh) mee-<u>eh</u>-doh

144. You're scaring me.   *Me estás asustando.*
Meh ess-<u>tahss</u> ah-soos-<u>tahn</u>-doh

DATE & TIME

145.   What day is today?   *¿Qué día es (hoy)?*
      Keh <u>dee</u>-ah ess (oy)

146.   Today is Monday.   *Hoy es lunes.*   **Oy ess <u>loo</u>-ness**

Tuesday.	*martes.*	<u>mar</u>-tess
Wednesday.	*miércoles.*	mee-<u>ehr</u>-koh-less
Thursday.	*jueves.*	<u>hweh</u>-vess
Friday.	*viernes.*	vee-<u>ehr</u>-ness
Saturday.	*sábado.*	<u>sah</u>-bah-doh
Sunday.	*domingo.*	doh-<u>meen</u>-goh
my birthday.	*mi cumpleaños.*	mee koom-pleh-<u>ah</u>-nyohss

147.   What day is tomorrow/the day after tomorrow?
      ¿Qué día es mañana/pasado mañana?
      Keh <u>dee</u>-ah ess mah-<u>nyah</u>-nah/pah-<u>sah</u>-doh mah-<u>nyah</u>-nah

148.   What day was yesterday?   *¿Qué día fue ayer?*
      Keh <u>dee</u>-ah foo-<u>eh</u> ah-<u>yehr</u>

149.   What did you do last night?   *¿Qué hiciste anoche?*
      Keh ee-<u>sees</u>-teh ah-<u>noh</u>-cheh

150.   It's January.   *Es el mes de enero.*
      Ess el mess deh eh-<u>neh</u>-roh

February.	*febrero.*	feh-<u>breh</u>-roh
March.	*marzo.*	<u>mar</u>-soh
April.	*abril.*	ah-<u>breel</u>
May.	*mayo.*	<u>mah</u>-yoh
June.	*junio.*	<u>hoo</u>-nee-oh
July.	*julio.*	<u>hoo</u>-lee-oh
August.	*agosto.*	ah-<u>gohs</u>-toh
September.	*septiembre.*	sep-tee-<u>em</u>-breh
October.	*octubre.*	ohk-<u>too</u>-breh
November.	*noviembre.*	noh-vee-<u>em</u>-breh
December.	*diciembre.*	dee-see-<u>em</u>-breh

151.   What's the date?   *¿Cuál es la fecha?*
       Kwahl ess lah <u>feh</u>-chah

152.   Today is Monday, January first.
       Hoy es lunes primero de enero.
       Oy ess <u>loo</u>-ness pree-<u>meh</u>-roh deh eh-<u>neh</u>-roh

153.   Next year I'm going to travel through Spain.
       El año próximo voy a viajar por España.
       El <u>ah</u>-nyoh <u>prohk</u>-see-moh voy ah vee-ah-<u>har</u> por Ess-<u>pah</u>-nyah

154.   Last year I went to Mexico.
       El año pasado fui a México.
       El <u>ah</u>-nyoh pah-<u>sah</u>-doh <u>fwee</u> ah <u>Meh</u>-hee-koh

155.   What time is it?   *¿Qué hora es?*   Keh <u>oh</u>-rah ess

156.   It's one/It's two o'clock in the morning.
       Es la una/Son las dos de la mañana.
       Ess la <u>oo</u>-nah/Sohn lahss dohss deh lah mah-<u>nyah</u>-nah

       in the afternoon/evening.   *de la tarde.*   deh lah <u>tar</u>-deh

157.   It's eight o'clock at night.   *Son las ocho de la noche.*
       Sohn lahss <u>oh</u>-choh deh lah <u>noh</u>-cheh

158.   It's nine-twenty.   *Son las nueve y veinte.*
       Sohn lahss <u>nweh</u>-veh ee <u>vayn</u> teh

159.   It's a quarter past ten.   *Son las diez y cuarto.*
       Sohn lahss dee-<u>ess</u> ee <u>kwar</u>-toh

160.   It's (very) early/late.   *Es (muy) temprano/tarde.*
       Ess (mooy) tem-<u>prah</u>-noh/<u>tar</u>-deh

161.   I need to wake up at . . .   *Necesito despertarme a las . . .*
       Neh-seh-<u>see</u>-toh dess-pehr-<u>tar</u>-meh ah lahss

162.   I must leave at . . . at the latest.
       Debo salir a más tardar a las . . .
       <u>Deh</u>-boh sah-<u>leer</u> ah mahss tar-<u>dar</u> ah lahss

163.   I have to leave in a few minutes.
       Me tengo que ir dentro de unos minutos.
       Meh <u>ten</u>-goh keh eer <u>den</u>-troh deh <u>oo</u>-nohss mee-<u>noo</u>-tohss

164. I want to get there early.   *Quiero llegar temprano.*
Kee-<u>eh</u>-roh yeh-<u>gar</u> tem-<u>prah</u>-noh

165. Hurry up. (for.)   *Dese prisa/apresúrese/apúrese.*
<u>Deh</u>-seh <u>pree</u>-sah/ah-preh-<u>soo</u>-reh-seh/ah-<u>poo</u>-reh-seh
Hurry up. (inf.)   *Date prisa/apresúrate/apúrate.*
<u>Dah</u>-teh <u>pree</u>-sah/ah-preh-<u>soo</u>-rah-teh/ah-<u>poo</u>-rah-teh

166. Let's go!   *¡Vamos!*   <u>Vah</u>-mohss

167. Fast!   *¡Rápido!*   <u>Rah</u>-pee-doh

168. I can't go any faster.   *No puedo ir más rápido.*
Noh <u>pweh</u>-doh eer mahss <u>rah</u>-pee-doh

169. We're running late.   *Vamos retrasados.*
<u>Vah</u>-mohss reh-trah-<u>sah</u>-dohss

170. Let's go next week.   *Vamos la semana próxima.*
<u>Vah</u>-mohss lah seh-<u>mah</u>-nah <u>prohk</u>-see-mah

CELEBRATIONS

171. When is your birthday?   *¿Cuándo es tu cumpleaños?*
<u>Kwahn</u>-doh ess too koom-pleh-<u>ah</u>-nyohss

172. Today is my birthday.   *Hoy es mi cumpleaños.*
Oy ess mee koom-pleh-<u>ah</u>-nyohss

173. Happy birthday!   *¡Feliz cumpleaños!*
Feh-<u>lees</u> koom-pleh-<u>ah</u>-nyohss

174. Many happy returns!   *¡Felicidades!*   Feh-lee-see-<u>dah</u>-dess

175. Congratulations!   *¡Felicitaciones!*
Feh-lee-see-tah-see-<u>oh</u>-ness

176. How old are you?   *¿Cuántos años cumples?*
<u>Kwahn</u>-tohss <u>ah</u>-nyohss <u>koom</u>-pless

177. What do you want as a present?   *¿Qué quieres de regalo?*
Keh kee-<u>eh</u>-ress deh reh-<u>gah</u>-loh

178. Let's go celebrate.   *Vamos a festejar.*
     Vah-mohss ah fess-teh-**hahr**

179. We just got married.   *Nos acabamos de casar.*
     Nohss ah-kah-**bah**-mohss deh kah-**sar**

180. We're having a baby.   *Vamos a tener un bebé.*
     Vah-mohss ah teh-**nehr** oon beh-**beh**

181. What holidays do you celebrate here?
     ¿Qué fiestas celebran aquí?
     Keh fee-**ess**-tahss seh-**leh**-brahn ah-**kee**

182. When is Independence Day?
     ¿Cuándo es el día de la independencia? (L. Am.)
     Kwahn-doh ess el **dee**-ah deh lah een-deh-pen-**den**-see-ah

183. When does Mardi Gras begin?
     ¿Cuándo empieza el carnaval?
     Kwahn-doh em-pee-**eh**-sah el kar-nah-**vahl**

184. When are the next holidays?
     ¿Cuándo son las próximas vacaciones?
     Kwahn-doh sohn lahss **prohk**-see-mahss vah-kah-see-**oh**-ness

185. Tonight is Christmas Eve.   *Esta noche es Noche Buena.*
     Ess-tah **noh**-cheh ess **noh**-cheh **bweh**-nah

186. Tomorrow is Christmas.   *Mañana es Navidad.*
     Mah-**nyah**-nah ess nah-vee-**dahd**

187. Merry Christmas!   *¡Feliz Navidad!*   Feh-**lees** nah-vee-**dahd**

188. Prosperous New Year!   *¡Próspero año nuevo!*
     Prohss-peh-roh **ah**-nyoh **nweh**-voh

189. Happy holidays!   *¡Felices fiestas!*
     Feh-**lee**-sess fee-**ess**-tahss

THE WEATHER

190. How's the weather?   *¿Cómo está el clima?*
     Koh-moh ess-**tah** el **klee**-mah

191. The weather's good/bad.
Hace buen/mal clima.
Ah-seh bwen/mahl **klee**-mah

192. It's (very) cloudy/sunny.
Está (muy) nublado/soleado.
Ess-**tah** (mooy) noo-**blah**-doh/soh-leh-**ah**-doh
dry/humid.   *seco/húmedo.*   **seh**-koh/**oo**-meh-doh

193. What's the temperature?
¿Cuál es la temperatura?
Kwahl ess lah tem-peh-rah-**too**-rah

194. It's (very) hot/cold.
Hace (mucho) calor/frío.
Ah-seh (-**moo**-choh) kah-**lor**/**free**-oh
windy.   *viento.*   vee-**en**-toh

195. It looks like it's going to rain.
Parece que va a llover.
Pah-**reh**-seh keh vah ah yoh-**vehr**

196. The sky is getting cloudy.   *El cielo se está nublando.*
El see-**eh**-loh seh ess-**tah** noo-**blahn**-doh

197. Should I take an umbrella?   *¿Debo llevar un paraguas?*
Deh-boh yeh-**var** oon par-**ah**-wahss

198. It's raining.   *Está lloviendo.*   Ess-**tah** yoh-vee-**en**-doh

199. A storm is approaching.   *Se acerca una tormenta.*
Seh ah-**sehr**-kah **oo**-nah tor-**men**-tah

200. A thunderstorm?   *¿Una tormenta eléctrica?*
Oo-nah tor-**men**-tah eh-**lek**-tree-kah

201. There's thunder and lightning.   *Hay rayos y truenos.*
I **rah**-yohss ee **trweh**-nohss

202. Tomorrow will be clear/rainy/stormy.
Mañana estará despejado/lluvioso/tormentoso.
Mah-**nyah**-nah ess-tah-**rah** dess-peh-**hah**-doh/
yoo-vee-**ohss**-oh/tor-men-**toh**-soh

GETTING THERE

203.   Where is the airport?   *¿Dónde está el aeropuerto?*
<u>Dohn</u>-deh ess-<u>tah</u> el I-roh-<u>pwehr</u>-toh

the train station?   *la estación del tren?*
lah ess-tah-see-<u>ohn</u> del tren

204.   Are we near/far from the port?
¿Estamos cerca/lejos del puerto?
Ess-<u>tah</u>-mohss <u>sehr</u>-kah/<u>leh</u>-hohss del <u>pwehr</u>-toh

the bus stop/terminal?   *de la parada/terminal de autobuses?*
deh lah pah-<u>rah</u>-dah /tehr-mee-<u>nahl</u> deh ow-toh-<u>boo</u>-sess

205.   I need to take the next flight to . . .
Necesito tomar el próximo vuelo a . . .
Neh-seh-<u>see</u>-toh toh-<u>mahr</u> el <u>prohk</u>-see-moh <u>vweh</u>-loh ah

the first/last flight to . . .   *el primer/último vuelo a . . .*
el pree-<u>mehr</u>/<u>ool</u>-tee-moh <u>vweh</u>-loh ah

206.   At what time does the flight coming from . . . arrive?
¿A qué hora llega el vuelo que viene de . . . ?
Ah keh <u>oh</u>-rah <u>yeh</u>-gah el <u>vweh</u>-loh keh vee-<u>eh</u>-neh deh

207.   Do you have the arrival/departure schedule? (for.)
¿Tiene el horario de salidas/llegadas?
Tee-<u>eh</u>-neh el oh-<u>rah</u>-ree-oh deh sahl-<u>ee</u>-dahss/yeh-<u>gah</u>-dahss

208.   Where is the ticket counter?
¿Dónde está la taquilla?   <u>Dohn</u>-deh ess-<u>tah</u> lah tah-<u>kee</u>-yah

the waiting area?   *la sala de espera?*
lah <u>sah</u>-lah deh ess-<u>peh</u>-rah

the departure gate?
la puerta de embarque?
lah <u>pwehr</u>-tah deh em-<u>bar</u>-keh

209.   What's the train platform number?
¿Cuál es el número del andén?
Kwahl ess el <u>noo</u>-meh-roh del ahn-<u>den</u>

the dock number?   *el número del muelle?*
el <u>noo</u>-meh-roh del <u>mweh</u>-yeh

210. How much is a ticket to . . . ?
¿Cuánto cuesta el boleto a . . . ?
Kwahn-toh **kwess**-tah el boh-**leh**-toh ah

  a ticket to . . . ?   *el billete a . . . ? (Sp.)*   el bee-**yeh**-teh ah

211. How many stops/transfers are there?
¿Cuántas paradas/cuántos cambios hay?
Kwahn-tahss pah-**rah**-das/**kwahn**-tohss **kahm**-bee-ohss I

212. How long does it take to get to . . . ?
¿Cuánto tarda en llegar a . . . ?
Kwahn-toh **tar**-dah en yeh-**gar** ah

213. Is there a discount for students?
¿Hay descuento para estudiantes?
I dess-**kwen**-toh **pah**-rah ess-too-dee-**ahn**-tess

  for teachers?   *para profesores?*
  pah-rah proh-feh-**soh**-ress

  for the elderly?   *para personas mayores?*
  pah-rah pehr-**sohn**-ahss mah-**yoh**-ress

214. Does it include travelers' insurance?
¿Incluye seguro de viajero?
Een-**kloo**-yeh seh-**goo**-roh deh vee-ah-**heh**-roh

215. I want a round trip ticket.
Quiero un boleto/billete de ida y vuelta.
Kee-**eh**-roh oon boh-**leh**-toh/bee-**yeh**-teh de **ee**-dah ee **vwel**-tah

  a one-way ticket.   *de ida solamente.*
  deh **ee**-dah soh-lah-**men**-teh

216. I would like a seat in the smoking/-non-smoking section.
Me gustaría un asiento en la sección de fumar/de no fumar.
Meh goos-tah-**ree**-ah oon ah-see-**en**-toh en lah sek-see-**ohn** deh
foo-**mar**/deh noh foo-**mar**

217. Do I need to make a reservation?
¿Necesito hacer una reservación?
Neh-seh-**see**-toh ah-**sehr** **oo**-nah reh-sehr-vah-see-**ohn**

218. I want to reserve a seat/two seats.
Quiero reservar un asiento/dos asientos.
Kee-**eh**-roh reh-sehr-**var** oon ah-see-**en**-toh/dohss ah-see-**en**-tohss

219. Does it leave on time?   *¿Sale puntualmente?*
    <u>Sah</u>-leh poon-twahl-<u>men</u>-teh

220. At what time can we board?
    ¿A qué hora podemos abordar/embarcar?
    Ah keh <u>oh</u>-rah poh-<u>deh</u>-mohss ah-bor-<u>dar</u>/em-bar-<u>kar</u>

221. Is this the train/bus that goes to . . . ?
    ¿Éste es el tren/autobús que va a . . . ?
    <u>Ess</u>-teh ess el tren/-ow-toh-<u>boos</u> keh vah ah

222. May I sit here?   *¿Me puedo sentar aquí?*
    Meh <u>pweh</u>-doh sen-<u>tar</u> ah-<u>kee</u>

223. Do you mind if I open the window? (for.)
    ¿Le importa si abro la ventanilla?
    Leh eem-<u>por</u>-tah see <u>ah</u>-broh lah ven-tah-<u>nee</u>-yah

224. Should I get off here?   *¿Debo bajar aquí?*
    <u>Deh</u>-boh bah-<u>har</u> ah-<u>kee</u>

225. My luggage was damaged.   *Se dañó mi equipaje.*
    Seh dah-<u>nyoh</u> mee eh-kee-<u>pah</u>-heh

226. Where's my luggage?   *¿Dónde está mi equipaje?*
    <u>Dohn</u>-deh ess-<u>tah</u> mee eh-kee-<u>pah</u>-heh

227. My luggage is missing/lost.   *Mi equipaje está perdido.*
    Mee eh-kee-<u>pah</u>-heh ess-<u>tah</u> pehr-<u>dee</u>-doh

228. My suitcase was stolen.   *Me robaron la maleta.*
    Meh roh-<u>bah</u>-rohn lah mah-<u>leh</u>-tah

GETTING ORIENTED

229. How do I get to . . . ?   *¿Cómo llego a . . . ?*
    <u>Koh</u>-moh <u>yeh</u>-goh ah

230. I want to go to . . .   *Quiero ir a . . .*   Kee-<u>eh</u>-roh eer ah

231. I'm looking for . . .   *Estoy buscando . . .*
    Ess-<u>toy</u> boos-<u>kahn</u>-doh

232. Do you know the address of . . . ? ¿Sabe la dirección de . . . ?
Sah-beh lah dee-rek-see-ohn deh

233. I need a (city/area) map.
Necesito un mapa (de la ciudad/del área).
Neh-seh-see-toh oon mah-pah (deh lah see-oo-dahd/del ah-reh-ah)

234. We need directions to get to . . .
Necesitamos direcciones para llegar a . . .
Neh-seh-see-tah-mohss dee-rek-see-oh-ness pah-rah yeh-gahr ah

235. How far is . . . ? ¿Qué tan lejos está . . . ?
Keh tahn leh-hohss ess-tah

236. Where is . . . ? ¿Dónde está . . . ? Dohn-deh ess-tah

237. Where are we? ¿Dónde estamos?
Dohn-deh ess-tah-mohss

238. Can you show me on the map? (for.)
¿Puede señalarlo en el mapa?
Pweh-deh seh-nyah-lar-loh en el mah-pah

239. Do I turn right/left?
¿Doy vuelta a la derecha/izquierda?
Doy vwel-tah ah lah deh-reh-chah/ees-kee-ehr-dah

    turn at the corner? en la esquina? en lah ess-kee-nah

    turn at the light? en el semáforo? en el sem-ah-foh-roh

240. How many streets/city blocks are there left to go?
¿Cuántas calles/cuadras faltan?
Kwahn-tahss kah-yess/-kwah-drahss fahl-tahn

241. Is the museum near/far? ¿Está cerca/lejos el museo?
Ess-tah sehr-kah/leh-hohss el moo-seh-oh

242. Can we walk there?
¿Podemos caminar hasta allá?
Poh-deh-mohss kah-mee-nahr ahss-tah ah-yah

GETTING AROUND

243. How can I get to . . . ?   *¿Cómo puedo llegar a . . . ?*
<u>Koh</u>-moh <u>pweh</u>-doh yeh-<u>gar</u> ah

244. What's the best way to go to . . . ?
¿Cuál es la mejor manera de ir a . . . ?
Kwahl ess lah meh-<u>hor</u> mah-<u>neh</u>-rah deh eer ah

245. Can you go on foot/walking?
¿Se puede ir a pie/caminando?
Seh <u>pweh</u>-deh eer ah pee-<u>eh</u>/kah-mee-<u>nahn</u>-doh

246. Can I get there by bus?   *¿Puedo llegar ahí en autobús?*
<u>Pweh</u>-doh yeh-<u>gar</u> ah-<u>ee</u> en ow-toh-<u>boos</u>

247. Is it complicated to go on the subway?
¿Es complicado ir en metro?
Ess kohm-plee-<u>kah</u>-doh eer en <u>meh</u>-troh

248. Is it better to take a taxi?   *¿Es mejor tomar un taxi?*
Ess meh-<u>hor</u> toh-<u>mar</u> oon <u>tah</u>-ksee

249. Where can I get a taxi?   *¿Dónde puedo conseguir un taxi?*
<u>Dohn</u>-deh <u>pweh</u>-doh kohn-seh-<u>geer</u> oon <u>tah</u>-ksee

250. Is it safe to take a taxi?   *¿Es seguro tomar un taxi?*
Ess seh-<u>goo</u>-roh toh-<u>mar</u> oon <u>tah</u>-ksee

251. Can you call a taxi for me? (for./inf.)
¿Puede(s) llamarme un taxi?
<u>Pweh</u>-deh(s) yah-<u>mar</u>-meh oon <u>tah</u>-ksee

252. I need a taxi at eight . . .   *Necesito un taxi a las ocho . . .*
Neh-seh-<u>see</u>-toh oon <u>tah</u>-ksee ah lahss <u>oh</u>-choh

253. Can you pick me up at . . . ? (for./inf.)
¿Puede(s) pasar por mí a las . . . ?
<u>Pweh</u>-deh(s) pah-<u>sar</u> por mee ah lahss

254. Are you available? (for.)   *¿Está libre?*   Ess-<u>tah</u> <u>lee</u>-breh

255. How much is it to go to the airport?
¿Cuánto cuesta ir al aeropuerto?
<u>Kwahn</u>-toh <u>kwess</u>-tah eer ahl I-roh-<u>pwehr</u>-toh

to the hotel?   *al hotel?*   ahl oh-<u>tel</u>

to the downtown area?   *al centro?*   ahl <u>sen</u>-troh

to this address?   *a esta dirección?*
ah <u>ess</u>-tah dee-rek-see-<u>ohn</u>

256. Do you charge by time or by distance?
¿Cobra por tiempo o por distancia?
<u>Koh</u>-brah por tee-<u>em</u>-poh oh por dees-<u>tahn</u>-see-ah

257. Please, take me to the train station. (for.)
Por favor, lléveme a la estación de tren.
Por fah-<u>vor</u>, <u>yeh</u>-veh-meh ah lah ess-tah-see-<u>ohn</u> deh tren

to the bus terminal.   *a la terminal de autobuses.*
ah lah tehr-mee-<u>nahl</u> deh ow-toh-<u>boo</u>-sess

to the hospital.   *al hospital.*   ahl ohss-pee-<u>tahl</u>

258. Is the meter working?   *¿Funciona el taxímetro?*
foon-see-<u>ohn</u>-ah el tahk-<u>see</u>-meh-troh

259. Drive slower/faster, please. (for.)
Vaya más despacio/rápido, por favor.
<u>Vah</u>-yah mahss dess-<u>pah</u>-see-oh/<u>rah</u>-pee-doh, por fah-<u>vor</u>

260. I'm (not) in a hurry.   *(No) Tengo prisa.*
(Noh) <u>Ten</u>-goh <u>pree</u>-sah

261. Stop at the corner. (for.)   *Pare en la esquina.*
<u>Pah</u>-reh en lah ess-<u>kee</u>-nah

262. Let me out here, please. (for.)
Déjeme aquí, por favor.   <u>Deh</u>-heh-meh ah-<u>kee</u>, por fah-<u>vor</u>

263. Can you wait for me here? (for.)
¿Me puede esperar aquí?   Meh <u>pweh</u>-deh ess-peh-<u>rar</u> ah-<u>kee</u>

264. Wait for me here, please (for.)   *Espéreme aquí, por favor.*
Ess-<u>peh</u>-reh-meh ah-<u>kee</u>, por fah-<u>vor</u>

265.   Can you take me back? (for.)   *¿Me puede llevar de regreso?*
        Meh <u>pweh</u>-deh yeh-<u>var</u> deh reh-<u>greh</u>-soh

266.   Keep the change. (for.)   *Quédese con el cambio.*
        <u>Keh</u>-deh-seh kohn el <u>kahm</u>-bee-oh

267.   Where is the bus stop?
        ¿Dónde está la parada del autobús?
        <u>Dohn</u>-deh ess-<u>tah</u> lah pah-<u>rah</u>-dah del ow-toh-<u>boos</u>

268.   Does the bus to . . . stop here?   *¿Para aquí el autobús a . . . ?*
        <u>Pah</u>-rah ah-<u>kee</u> el ow-toh-<u>boos</u> ah

269.   What's the fare?   *¿Cuánto cuesta el pasaje?*
        <u>Kwahn</u>-toh <u>kwess</u>-tah el pah-<u>sah</u>-heh

270.   What's the nearest subway station?
        ¿Cuál es la estación de metro más cercana?
        Kwahl ess lah ess-tah-see-<u>ohn</u> deh <u>meh</u>-troh mahss
        sehr-<u>kah</u>-nah

271.   Where can I buy a ticket?
        ¿Dónde puedo comprar un boleto?
        <u>Dohn</u>-deh <u>pweh</u>-doh kohm-<u>prar</u> oon boh-<u>leh</u>-toh

272.   One ticket, please.   *Un boleto, por favor.*
        Oon boh-<u>leh</u>-toh por fah-<u>vor</u>

273.   (Where) Must I transfer to get to . . . ?
        ¿(Dónde) Debo transbordar para llegar a . . . ?
        (<u>Dohn</u>-deh) <u>Deh</u>-boh trahns-bor-<u>dar</u> <u>pah</u>-rah yeh-<u>gar</u> ah

274.   Where can I rent a car?
        ¿Dónde puedo alquilar/ rentar un auto?
        <u>Dohn</u>-deh <u>pweh</u>-doh ahl-kee-<u>lar</u>/ren-<u>tar</u> oon <u>ow</u>-toh

275.   I would like to rent a car (with air conditioning).
        Quisiera alquilar/rentar un auto (con aire acondicionado).
        Kee-see-<u>eh</u>-rah ahl-kee-<u>lar</u>/ren-<u>tar</u> oon <u>ow</u>-toh (kohn <u>I</u>-reh
        ah-kohn-dee-see-oh-<u>nah</u>-doh)

276.   How much is the rate per hour/day/week?
        ¿Cuánto cuesta el alquiler por hora/día/semana?
        <u>Kwahn</u>-toh <u>kwess</u>-tah el ahl-kee-<u>lehr</u> por <u>oh</u>-rah/<u>dee</u>-ah/
        seh-<u>mah</u>-nah

277. Does it include insurance?   *¿Incluye seguro?*
Een-<u>kloo</u>-yeh seh-<u>goo</u>-roh

278. Do you have a highway/city map? (for.)
¿Tiene un mapa de carreteras/de la ciudad?
Tee-<u>eh</u>-neh oon <u>mah</u>-pah deh kah-reh-<u>teh</u>-rahss/deh lah
<u>see</u>-oo-dahd

279. What's the speed limit?   *¿Cuál es el límite de velocidad?*
Kwahl ess el <u>lee</u>-mee-teh deh vel-oh-see-<u>dahd</u>

280. Do you know where there's a parking lot? (for.)
¿Sabe dónde hay un estacionamiento?
<u>Sah</u>-beh <u>dohn</u>-deh I oon ess-tah-see-oh-nah-mee-<u>en</u>-toh

281. What's the rate?   *¿Cuál es la tarifa?*
Kwahl ess lah tah-<u>ree</u>-fah

282. Do you charge by the hour/fraction of an hour?
¿Cobran por hora/por fracción?
<u>Koh</u>-brahn por <u>oh</u>-rah/por frahk-see-<u>ohn</u>

283. Can I park here?   *¿Puedo estacionarme aquí?*
<u>Pweh</u>-doh ess-tah-see-oh-<u>nar</u>-meh ah-<u>kee</u>

284. Do I need to put coins in the parking meter?
¿Necesito poner monedas en el parquímetro?
Neh-seh-<u>see</u>-toh poh-<u>nehr</u> moh-<u>neh</u>-dahss en el
par-<u>kee</u>-meh-troh

285. I don't want to get a ticket.
No quiero que me pongan una multa.
Noh kee-<u>eh</u>-roh keh meh <u>pohn</u>-gahn <u>oo</u>-nah <u>mool</u>-tah

286. Where is there a gas station around here?
¿Dónde hay una gasolinera por aquí?
<u>Dohn</u>-deh I <u>oo</u>-nah gah-soh-lee-<u>neh</u>-rah por ah-<u>kee</u>

287. Fill it up, please.   *Lleno, por favor.*   <u>Yeh</u>-noh, por fah-<u>vor</u>

288. Can you check the oil? (for.)
¿Puede checar el aceite?
<u>Pweh</u>-deh cheh-<u>kar</u> el ah-<u>say</u>-teh

the tire pressure?   *la presión?*   lah preh-see-<u>ohn</u>

A PLACE TO STAY

289. I want to stay in a (cheap/fancy) hotel.
Quiero hospedarme en un hotel (barato/de lujo).
Kee-<u>eh</u>-roh ohss-peh-<u>dar</u>-meh en oon oh-<u>tel</u> (bah-<u>rah</u>-toh/deh <u>loo</u>-hoh)

a hotel near the downtown area.   *un hotel cerca del centro.*
oon oh-<u>tel</u> <u>sehr</u>-kah del <u>sen</u>-troh

a bed-and-breakfast.   *una pensión con desayuno.*
<u>oo</u>-nah pen-see-<u>ohn</u> kohn deh-sah-<u>yoo</u>-noh

290. How much is a room per night?
¿Cuánto cuesta la habitación por noche?
<u>Kwahn</u>-toh <u>kwess</u>-tah lah ah-bee-tah-see-<u>ohn</u> por <u>noh</u>-cheh

per week?   *por semana?*   por seh-<u>mah</u>-nah

per person?   *por persona?*   por pehr-<u>soh</u>-<u>nah</u>

291. Does it include meals?   *¿Incluye comidas?*
Een-<u>kloo</u>-yeh koh-<u>mee</u>-dahss

breakfast?   *el desayuno?*   el deh-sah-<u>yoo</u>-noh

dinner?   *la cena?*   lah <u>seh</u>-nah

292. I have a reservation.   *Tengo una reservación.*
<u>Ten</u>-goh <u>oo</u>-nah reh-sehr-vah-see-<u>ohn</u>

293. Can I make a reservation (for today)?
¿Puedo hacer una reservación (para hoy)?
<u>Pweh</u>-doh ah-<u>sehr</u> <u>oo</u>-nah reh-sehr-vah-see-<u>ohn</u> (-<u>pah</u>-rah oy)

294. I want to make a reservation for tomorrow.
Quiero hacer una reservación para mañana.
Kee-<u>eh</u>-roh ah-<u>ser</u> <u>oo</u>-nah reh-sehr-vah-see-<u>ohn</u> <u>pah</u>-rah mah-<u>nyah</u>-nah

for next week.   *para la semana próxima.*
<u>pah</u>-rah lah seh-<u>mah</u>-nah <u>prohk</u>-see-mah

295. Do you have rooms available? (for.)
¿Tiene habitaciones disponibles?
Tee-<u>eh</u>-neh ah-bee-tah-see-<u>oh</u>-ness dees-poh-<u>nee</u>-bless

296. I would like a single/double room.
      Quisiera una habitación sencilla/doble.
      Kee-see-<u>eh</u>-rah <u>oo</u>-nah ah-bee-tah-see-<u>ohn</u> sen-<u>see</u>-yah/<u>doh</u>-bleh

      a room with a bathroom/bathtub.
      una habitación con baño/tina.
      <u>oo</u>-nah ah-bee-tah-see-<u>ohn</u> kohn <u>bah</u>-nyoh/<u>tee</u>-nah

297. I want a room with air conditioning.
      Quiero una habitación con aire acondicionado.
      **Kee-<u>eh</u>-roh <u>oo</u>-nah ah-bee-tah-see-<u>ohn</u> kohn <u>I</u>-reh
      ah-kohn-dee-see-oh-<u>nah</u>-doh**

298. May I see the room?   *¿Puedo ver la habitación?*
      <u>Pweh</u>-doh vehr lah ah-bee-tah-see-<u>ohn</u>

299. Does it have hot water?   *¿Tiene agua caliente?*
      Tee-<u>eh</u>-neh <u>ah</u>-wah kah-lee-<u>en</u>-teh

      cable TV?   *televisión con cable?*
      teh-leh-vee-see-<u>ohn</u> kohn <u>kah</u>-bleh

      Internet access?   *conexión a la red?*
      koh-nek-see-<u>ohn</u> ah lah red

      Wi-Fi?   *conexión inalámbrica?*
      koh-nek-see-<u>ohn</u> een-ah-<u>lahm</u>-bree-kah

      kitchenette?   *cocineta?*   **koh-see-<u>neh</u>-tah**

300. Is there laundry service?   *¿Hay servicio de lavandería?*
      I sehr-<u>vee</u>-see-oh de lah-vahn-deh-<u>ree</u>-ah

      parking?   *estacionamiento?*
      ess-tah-see-oh-nah-mee-<u>en</u>-toh

301. I will be staying for one night/two nights.
      Me voy a quedar una noche/dos noches.
      Meh voy ah keh-<u>dar</u> <u>oo</u>-nah <u>noh</u>-cheh/dohss <u>noh</u>-chess

      one week/two weeks.   *una semana/dos semanas.*
      <u>oo</u>-nah seh-<u>mah</u>-nah/dohss seh-<u>mah</u>-nahss

302. I don't know how long I will be staying.
      No sé por cuánto tiempo me voy a quedar.
      Noh seh por <u>kwahn</u>-toh tee-<u>em</u>-poh meh voy ah keh-<u>dar</u>

303.   I want to stay another night.
       Quiero quedarme una noche más.
       Kee-<u>eh</u>-roh keh-<u>dar</u>-meh <u>oo</u>-nah <u>noh</u>-cheh mahss

304.   Do you take credit cards?
       ¿Aceptan tarjetas de crédito?
       Ah-<u>sep</u>-tahn tar-<u>heh</u>-tahs deh <u>kreh</u>-dee-toh

       cash?   *efectivo?*   **-eh-fek-<u>tee</u>-voh**

305.   Is there a strong box in the room?
       ¿Hay una caja de seguridad en la habitación?
       **I <u>oo</u>-nah <u>kah</u>-hah deh seh-<u>goo</u>-ree-dahd en lah
       ah-bee-tah-see-<u>ohn</u>**

306.   Should I leave my valuables at the desk?
       ¿Debo dejar mis objetos de valor en la recepción?
       **<u>Deh</u>-boh deh-<u>hahr</u> mees ohb-<u>heh</u>-tohss deh vah-<u>lor</u> en lah
       reh-sep-see-<u>ohn</u>**

307.   Can somebody help me with my luggage?
       ¿Me puede ayudar alguien con mis maletas?
       **Meh <u>pweh</u>-deh ah-yoo-<u>dar</u> <u>ahl</u>-gee-en kohn mees
       mah-<u>leh</u>-tahss**

308.   By what time do I need to check out?
       ¿A qué hora debo dejar libre la habitación?
       **Ah keh <u>oh</u>-rah <u>deh</u>-boh deh-<u>har</u> <u>lee</u>-breh lah
       ah-bee-tah-see-<u>ohn</u>**

309.   At what time do you serve breakfast/dinner?
       ¿A qué hora sirven el desayuno/la cena?
       Ah keh <u>oh</u>-rah <u>seer</u>-ven el deh-sah-<u>yoo</u>-noh/lah <u>seh</u>-nah

310.   Until what time do you serve breakfast/dinner?
       Hasta qué hora sirven el desayuno/la cena?
       <u>Ahss</u>-tah keh <u>oh</u>-rah <u>seer</u>-ven el deh-sah-<u>yoo</u>-noh/lah <u>seh</u>-nah

311.   Can you wake me up at . . . ?   *¿Me puede despertar a las . . . ?*
       Meh <u>pweh</u>-deh dess-pehr-<u>tar</u> ah lahss

312.   Where is the elevator?   *¿Dónde está el ascensor/elevador?*
       <u>Dohn</u>-deh ess-<u>tah</u> el ah-sen-<u>sor</u>/el-eh-vah-<u>dor</u>

       the dining room?   *el comedor?*   **el koh-meh-<u>dor</u>**

313. Is there a workout room?
     ¿Hay un cuarto de ejercicios?
     I oon **kwar**-toh deh eh-hehr-<u>see</u>-see-ohss

     a swimming pool?   *una piscina/alberca?*
     <u>oo</u>-nah pee-<u>see</u>-nah/ahl-<u>behr</u>-kah

     a business center?   *un centro de negocios?*
     oon <u>sen</u>-troh deh neh-<u>goh</u>-see-ohss

314. Can you clean the room now/later? (for.)
     ¿Puede asear la habitación ahora/más tarde?
     <u>Pweh</u>-deh ah-seh-<u>ar</u> lah ah-bee-tah-see-<u>ohn</u> ah-<u>oh</u>-rah/ mahss <u>tar</u>-deh

315. These sheets are dirty.   *Estas sábanas están sucias.*
     <u>Ess</u>-tahss <u>sah</u>-bah-nahss ess-<u>tahn</u> <u>soo</u>-see-ahss

316. I need clean sheets.   *Necesito sábanas limpias.*
     Neh-seh-<u>see</u>-toh <u>sah</u>-bah-nahss <u>leem</u>-pee-ahss

     clean towels.   *toallas limpias.*   <u>twah</u>-yahss <u>leem</u>-pee-ahss

     another blanket.   *otra cobija/manta.*
     <u>oh</u>-trah koh-<u>bee</u>-hah/<u>mahn</u>-tah

317. Can you bring me another pillow? (for.)
     ¿Me puede traer otra almohada/cojín?
     Meh <u>pweh</u>-deh trah-<u>ehr</u> <u>oh</u>-trah ahl-moh-<u>ah</u>-dah/koh-<u>heen</u>

     an extra bed?   *una cama extra?*   <u>oo</u>-nah <u>kah</u>-mah <u>ek</u>-strah

318. How does the heat work?
     ¿Cómo funciona la calefacción?
     <u>Koh</u>-moh foon-see-<u>oh</u>-nah lah kah-leh-fahk-see-<u>ohn</u>

     the air conditioning work?   *el aire acondicionado?*
     el <u>I</u>-reh ah-kohn-dee-see-oh-<u>nah</u>-doh

319. I lost my key.   *Perdí mi llave.*   -Pehr-<u>dee</u> mee <u>yah</u>-veh

320. My room number is . . .   *Mi número de cuarto es . . .*
     Mee <u>noo</u>-meh-roh deh <u>kwar</u>-toh ess

321. I'm leaving.   *Ya me voy.*   Yah meh voy

322. The bill, please.   *La cuenta, por favor.*
     Lah <u>kwen</u>-tah, por fah-<u>vor</u>

323. I think there is a mistake in the bill.
Creo que hay un error en la cuenta.
Kreh-oh keh I oon eh-**ror** en lah **kwen**-tah

324. I didn't make these calls.   *Yo no hice estas llamadas.*
Yoh noh **ee**-seh **ess**-tahss yah-**mah**-dahss

325. I want to rent an apartment.
Quiero rentar/alquilar un apartamento.
Kee-**eh**-roh ren-**tar**/ahl-kee-**lar** oon ah-par-tah-**men**-toh

an (a furnished) apartment.   *un piso (amueblado). (Sp.)*
oon **pee**-soh (ah-mweh-**blah**-doh)

a cabin.   *una cabaña.*   **oo**-nah kah-**bah**-nyah

a house.   *una casa.*   **oo**-nah **kah**-sah

326. How many rooms/bathrooms does it have?
¿Cuántos cuartos/baños tiene?
Kwahn-tohss **kwar**-tohss/**bah**-nyohss tee-**eh**-neh

327. Do I need to give a deposit?   *¿Necesito dar un depósito?*
Neh-seh-**see**-toh dar oon deh-**poh**-see-toh

EATING & DRINKING

328. I'm (not) (very) hungry.   *(No) Tengo (mucha) hambre.*
(Noh) **Ten**-goh (-**moo**-chah) **ahm**-breh

thirsty.   *sed.*   sehd

329. I want to eat/drink (something).   *Quiero comer/beber (algo).*
Kee-**eh**-roh koh-**mehr**/beh-**behr** (-**ahl**-goh)

330. When can we eat?   *¿Cúando podemos comer?*
Kwahn-doh poh-**deh**-mohss koh-**mehr**

331. It's time for breakfast.   *Es hora de desayunar.*
Ess **oh**-rah deh deh-sah-yoo-**nar**

for an early lunch.   *de almorzar.*   deh ahl-mor-**sar**

for lunch.   *de comer.*   deh koh-**mehr**

332. I feel like eating an early dinner.   *Tengo ganas de merendar.*
Ten-goh **gah**-nahss deh meh-ren-**dar**

dinner.   *de cenar.*   deh seh-**nar**

a snack.   *de un tentempié.*   deh oon ten-tem-pee-**eh**

333.   Can you recommend a (good) restaurant? (for.)
       ¿Me puede recomendar un (buen) restaurante?
       Meh <u>pweh</u>-deh reh-koh-men-<u>dar</u> oon bwen ress-tow-<u>rahn</u>-teh

       a (good) snack bar?   *una (buena) cafetería?*
       <u>oo</u>-nah (-<u>bweh</u>-nah) kah-feh-teh-<u>ree</u>-ah

       a (good) coffee shop?   *un (buen) café?*   oon (bwen) kah-<u>feh</u>

       a (good) bar?   *un (buen) bar?*   oon (bwen) bar

334.   I would like to try the local food.
       Me gustaría probar la comida típica.
       Meh goos-tah-<u>ree</u>-ah proh-<u>bar</u> lah koh-<u>mee</u>-dah <u>tee</u>-pee-kah

335.   I want to go to a fast food restaurant.
       Quiero ir a un restaurante de comida rápida.
       Kee-<u>eh</u>-roh eer ah oon ress-tow-<u>rahn</u>-teh deh koh-<u>mee</u>-dah
       <u>rah</u>-pee-dah

336.   I am looking for a cheap/expensive restaurant.
       Estoy buscando un restaurante barato/caro.
       Ess-<u>toy</u> boos-<u>kahn</u>-doh oon ress-tow-<u>rahn</u>-teh bah-<u>rah</u>-toh/
       <u>kah</u>-roh

337.   Do you know any vegetarian restaurants? (inf.)
       ¿Conoces algún restaurante vegetariano?
       Koh-<u>noh</u>-sess ahl-<u>goon</u> ress-tow-<u>rahn</u>-teh veh-heh-tah-ree-<u>ah</u>-noh

338.   What's the city's best restaurant?
       ¿Cuál es el mejor restaurante de la ciudad?
       Kwahl ess el meh-<u>hor</u> ress-tow-<u>rahn</u>-teh deh la <u>see</u>-oo-dahd

339.   Do you need a reservation?
       ¿Se necesita una reservación?
       Seh neh-seh-<u>see</u>-tah <u>oo</u>-nah reh-sehr-vah-see-<u>ohn</u>

340.   Will I need to wear a jacket?
       ¿Tendré que usar chaqueta/saco? (L. Am.)
       Ten-<u>dreh</u> keh oo-<u>sar</u> chah-<u>keh</u>-tah/<u>sah</u>-koh

341.   Let's go have [something before/after eating].
       Vamos a tomar algo antes/después de comer.
       <u>Vah</u>-mohss ah toh-<u>mar</u> <u>ahl</u>-goh <u>ahn</u>-tehss/dess-<u>pwess</u> deh
       koh-<u>mehr</u>

a drink.   *un trago.*   oon <u>trah</u>-goh

a beer.   *una cerveza.*   <u>oo</u>-nah sehr-<u>veh</u>-sah

a glass of wine.   *una copa de vino.*
<u>oo</u>-nah <u>koh</u>-pah deh <u>vee</u>-noh

red wine mixed with fruit and lemonade.
una sangría. (Sp.)   <u>oo</u>-nah sahn-<u>gree</u>-ah

a drink before lunch.   *un aperitivo.*
oon ah-peh-ree-<u>tee</u>-voh

some coffee.   *un café.*   oon kah-<u>feh</u>

342. I want to try some traditional Spanish hors d'oeuvres.
Quiero probar unas tapas.
Kee-<u>eh</u>-roh proh-<u>bar</u> <u>oo</u>-nahss <u>tah</u>-pahss

343. We need a table for four (people).
Necesitamos una mesa para cuatro (personas).
Neh-seh-see-<u>tah</u>-mohss <u>oo</u>-nah <u>meh</u>-sah <u>pah</u>-rah <u>kwah</u>-troh
(per-<u>soh</u>-nahss)

a table in the (non) smoking section.
una mesa en la sección de (no) fumar.
<u>oo</u>-nah <u>meh</u>-sah en lah sek-see-<u>ohn</u> deh (noh) foo-<u>mar</u>

344. We want a table outside/inside.
Queremos una mesa afuera/adentro.
Keh-<u>reh</u>-mohss <u>oo</u>-nah <u>meh</u>-sah ah-<u>fweh</u>-rah/ah-<u>den</u>-troh

by the window.   *cerca de la ventana.*
<u>sehr</u>-cah deh lah ven-<u>tah</u>-nah

far from the kitchen.   *lejos de la cocina.*
<u>leh</u>-hohss deh lah koh-<u>see</u>-nah

345. Can we sit here?   *¿Nos podemos sentar aquí?*
Nohss poh-<u>deh</u>-mohss sen-<u>tar</u> ah-<u>kee</u>

346. I made a reservation.   *Hice una reservación.*
<u>Ee</u>-seh <u>oo</u>-nah reh-sehr-vah-see-<u>ohn</u>

347. Waiter! (lit. young man)   *¡Joven!*   <u>Hoh</u>-ven
Waiter!   *¡Camarero!*   Kah-mah-<u>reh</u>-roh

348. Miss!   *¡Señorita!*   Seh-nyoh-<u>ree</u>-tah

349. Can you bring us the menu?
      ¿Nos puede traer la carta/el menú?
      Nohss pweh-deh trah-ehr lah kar-tah/el meh-noo

      the wine list?   *la carta de vinos?*   lah kar-tah deh vee-nohss

      a children's menu?   *una carta/un menú para niños?*
      oo-nah kar-tah/oon meh-noo pah-rah nee-nyohss

350. Do you have a menu in English? (for.)
      ¿Tiene una carta/un menú en inglés?
      Tee-eh-neh oo-nah kar-tah/oon meh-noo en een-gless

351. We are ready to order.   *Estamos listos para ordenar.*
      Ess-tah-mohss lees-tohss pah-rah or-deh-nar

352. What do you recommend?   *¿Qué nos recomienda?*
      Keh nohss reh-koh-mee-en-dah

353. Do you have vegetarian dishes?   *¿Tiene platillos vegetarianos?*
      Tee-eh-neh plah-tee-yohss veh-heh-tah-ree-ah-nohss

      low-calorie dishes?   *bajos en calorías?*
      bah-hohss en kah-loh-ree-ahss

354. I need a (clean) napkin.   *Necesito una servilleta (limpia).*
      Neh-seh-see-toh oo-nah sehr-vee-yeh-tah (-leem-pee-ah)

      (clean) silverware.   *unos cubiertos (limpios).*
      oo-nohss koo-bee-ehr-tohss (-leem-pee-ohss)

      a spoon.   *una cuchara.*   oo-nah koo-chah-rah

      a fork.   *un tenedor.*   oon ten-eh-dor

      a knife.   *un cuchillo.*   oon koo-chee-yoh

      a teaspoon.   *una cucharita.*   oo-nah koo-chah-ree-tah

      more bread.   *más pan.*   mahss pahn

355. What do you want to eat for breakfast? (inf.)
      ¿Qué quieres desayunar?   Keh kee-eh-ress deh-sah-yoo-nar

356. For breakfast I would like cereal with milk.
      Para desayunar me gustaría cereal con leche.
      Pah-rah deh-sah-yoo-nar meh goos-tah-ree-ah seh-reh-ahl
      kohn leh-cheh

      oatmeal.   *avena.*   ah-veh-nah

toast (with butter and jam).
pan tostado (con mantequilla y mermelada).
**pahn tohss-<u>tah</u>-doh (kohn mahn-teh-<u>kee</u>-yah ee
mehr-meh-<u>lah</u>-dah)**

toast. *una tostada. (Sp.)* <u>oo</u>-nah tohss-<u>tah</u>-dah

pastries. *pan dulce.* **pahn <u>dool</u>-seh**

French toast. *pan francés.* **pahn frahn-<u>sess</u>**

pancakes. *panqueques. (L. Am.)* **pahn-<u>keh</u>-kess**

357. I will have a fresh fruit plate.
Tomaré un plato de fruta fresca.
Toh-mah-<u>reh</u> oon <u>plah</u>-toh deh <u>froo</u>-tah <u>fress</u>-kah

358. To drink, I would like coffee (decaf).
De tomar me gustaría un café (descafeinado).
**Deh toh-<u>mar</u> meh goos-tah-<u>ree</u>-ah un kah-<u>feh</u>
(dess-kah-fay-<u>nah</u>-doh)**

coffee with milk. *café con leche.* **kah-<u>feh</u> kohn
<u>leh</u>-cheh**

(black/chamomile) tea. *té (negro/de manzanilla).*
teh (-<u>neh</u>-groh/deh mahn-sah-<u>nee</u>-yah)

hot/cold chocolate. *chocolate caliente/frío.*
choh-koh-<u>lah</u>-teh kah-lee-<u>en</u>-teh/<u>free</u>-oh

a glass of milk. *un vaso de leche.*
oon <u>vah</u>-soh deh <u>leh</u>-cheh

orange juice. *jugo de naranja.*
<u>hoo</u>-goh deh nah-<u>rahn</u>-hah

orange juice. *zumo de naranja. (Sp.)*
<u>soo</u>-moh deh nah-<u>rahn</u>-hah

359. As a starter I would like the soup of the day.
Como primer plato quisiera la sopa del día.
**<u>Koh</u>-moh pree-<u>mehr</u> <u>plah</u>-toh kee-see-<u>eh</u>-rah lah <u>soh</u>-pah del
<u>dee</u>-ah**

vegetable soup. *sopa de verduras/legumbres. (Sp.)*
<u>soh</u>-pah de vehr-<u>doo</u>-rahss/<u>leh</u>-<u>goom</u>-bress

noodle soup. *sopa de fideos.* **<u>soh</u>-pah deh fee-<u>deh</u>-ohss**

lentil soup. *sopa de lentejas.* **<u>soh</u>-pah deh len-<u>teh</u>-hahss**

chicken broth (with rice).
caldo/consomé de pollo (con arroz).
<u>kahl</u>-doh/kohn-soh-<u>meh</u> deh <u>poh</u>-yoh (kohn ah-<u>rohss</u>)

rice.   *arroz.*   ah-<u>rohss</u>

meat-filled pastry.   *empanadas. (L. Am.)*
em-pah-<u>nah</u>-dahss

cold vegetable soup.   *gazpacho. (Sp.)*   gahss-<u>pah</u>-choh

360.   Bring me a (green/mixed) salad.
Tráigame una ensalada (verde/mixta).
<u>Tri</u>-gah-meh <u>oo</u>-nah en-sah-<u>lah</u>-dah (-<u>vehr</u>-deh/<u>meeks</u>-tah)

a cucumber salad.   *una ensalada de pepino.*
<u>oo</u>-nah en-sah-<u>lah</u>-dah deh peh-<u>pee</u>-noh

a tomato salad.   *una ensalada de tomate.*
<u>oo</u>-nah en-sah-<u>lah</u>-dah deh toh-<u>mah</u>-teh

361.   How's the chicken?   *¿Cómo está el pollo?*
<u>Koh</u>-moh ess-<u>tah</u> el <u>poh</u>-yoh

362.   As a main dish I would like grilled chicken.
Como plato principal quisiera pollo a la parrilla.
<u>Koh</u>-moh <u>plah</u>-toh preen-see-<u>pahl</u> kee-see-<u>eh</u>-rah <u>poh</u>-yoh ah
lah pah-<u>ree</u>-yah

fried chicken.   *pollo frito.*   <u>poh</u>-yoh <u>free</u>-toh

chicken breast.   *pechuga de pollo.*
peh-<u>choo</u>-gah de <u>poh</u>-yoh

chicken thigh and leg.   *pierna y muslo.*
pee-<u>ehr</u>-nah ee <u>moos</u>-loh

duck (in blackberry sauce).   *pato (en salsa de zarzamora).*
<u>pah</u>-toh (en <u>sahl</u>-sah deh sar-sah-<u>moh</u>-rah)

(stuffed) turkey.   *pavo (relleno).*   <u>pah</u>-voh (-reh-<u>yeh</u>-noh)

roast beef.   *carne asada.*   <u>kar</u>-neh ah-<u>sah</u>-dah

beef steak.   *bife. (Arg.)*   <u>bee</u>-feh

steak.   *solomillo. (Sp.)*   soh-loh-<u>mee</u>-yoh

363.   I prefer it cooked rare.
Lo prefiero medio rojo/poco hecho. (Sp.)
Loh preh-fee-<u>eh</u>-roh <u>meh</u>-dee-oh <u>roh</u>-hoh/<u>poh</u>-koh <u>eh</u>-choh

cooked medium.   *término medio/medio hecho. (Sp.)*
tehr-mee-noh **meh**-dee-oh/**meh**-dee-oh **eh**-choh

cooked well done.   *bien cocido/bien hecho. (Sp.)*
bee-**en** koh-**see**-doh/bee-**en eh**-choh

364.   I'll order meatballs.   *Pediré albóndigas.*
Peh-dee-**reh** ahl-**bohn**-dee-gahss

a hamburger.   *una hamburguesa.*
oo-nah ahm-boor-**geh**-sah

pork chop.   *chuleta de cerdo.*   choo-**leh**-tah deh **sehr**-doh

pork loin.   *lomo de cerdo.*   **loh**-moh deh **sehr**-doh

veal scallop.   *escalope de ternera.*
ess-kah-**loh**-peh deh tehr-**neh**-rah

rack of lamb.   *costillas de cordero.*
kohss-**tee**-yahss deh kor-**deh**-roh

365.   I think I'll have filet of fish.   *Creo que comeré filete de pescado.*
Kreh-oh keh koh-mehr-**eh** fee-**leh**-teh deh pes-**kah**-doh

fresh tuna fish.   *atún fresco.*   ah-**toon fress**-koh

cod fish.   *bacalao.*   bah-kah-**lah**-oh

sole fish.   *lenguado.*   len-**gwah**-doh

grouper fish.   *mero.*   **meh**-roh

red snapper.   *huachinango.*   wah-chee-**nahn**-goh

sea bass.   *robalo.*   roh-**bah**-loh

salmon.   *salmón.*   sahl-**mohn**

trout.   *trucha.*   **troo**-chah

366.   I would prefer the seafood dish.
Preferiría el plato de mariscos.
Preh-feh-ree-**ree**-ah el **plah**-toh deh mah-**rees**-kohss

mussels.   *mejillones.*   meh-hee-**yoh**-ness

shrimp.   *camarones/gambas.*
kah-mah-**roh**-ness/**gahm**-bahss

prawns.   *langostinos.*   lahn-gohss-**tee**-nohss

lobster.   *langosta.*   lahn-**gohss**-tah

squids (in ink).   *calamares (en su tinta).*
kah-lah-**mah**-ress

octopus.   *pulpo.*   **pool**-poh

367.   Is it very spicy?   *¿Es muy picante?*
       Ess mooy pee-<u>kahn</u>-teh

368.   Does it have a lot of fat?   *¿Tiene mucha grasa?*
       Tee-<u>eh</u>-neh <u>moo</u>-chah <u>grah</u>-sah

369.   No onions, please.   *Sin cebolla, por favor.*
       Seen seh-<u>boh</u>-yah por fah-<u>vor</u>

370.   Please do not add salt.   *Por favor no le ponga sal.*
       Por fah-<u>vor</u> noh leh <u>pohn</u>-gah sahl

371.   I'm allergic to nuts.   *Soy alérgico a las nueces.*
       Soy ah-<u>lehr</u>-hee-koh ah lahss <u>nweh</u>-sess

       to shellfish.   *a los mariscos.*   **ah lohss mah-<u>rees</u>-kohss**

372.   Is it served with French fries?   *¿Se sirve con papas fritas?*
       Seh <u>seer</u>-veh kohn <u>pah</u>-pahss <u>free</u>-tahss

       French fries?   *patatas fritas? (Sp.)*   **pah-<u>tah</u>-tahss <u>free</u>-tahss**

       a baked potato?   *una papa/patata al horno?*
       <u>oo</u>-nah <u>pah</u>-pah/pah-<u>tah</u>-tah ahl <u>ohr</u>-noh

       mashed potatoes?   *puré de papa/patata? (Sp.)*
       poo-<u>reh</u> deh <u>pah</u>-pah/pah-<u>tah</u>-tah

373.   What do you have to drink?   *¿Qué bebidas tienen?*
       Keh beh-<u>bee</u>-dahss tee-<u>eh</u>-nen

374.   Is the water filtered?   *¿Está filtrada el agua?*
       Ess-<u>tah</u> feel-<u>trah</u>-dah el <u>ah</u>-wah

375.   To drink, I want water.   *De tomar, quiero agua.*
       Deh toh-<u>mar</u>, kee-<u>eh</u>-roh <u>ah</u>-wah

       bottled water.   *agua embotellada.*
       <u>ah</u>-wah em-boh-teh-<u>yah</u>-dah

       mineral water.   *agua mineral.*   **<u>ah</u>-wah mee-neh-<u>rahl</u>**

       hibiscus-flower ice tea.   *agua de jamaica.*
       <u>ah</u>-wah deh hah-<u>mi</u>-kah

       a (light/dark) beer.   *una cerveza (clara/oscura).*
       <u>oo</u>-nah sehr-<u>veh</u>-sah (<u>klah</u>-rah/ohss-<u>koo</u>-rah)

       a glass of wine red/white.   *una copa de vino tinto/blanco.*
       <u>oo</u>-nah <u>koh</u>-pah deh <u>vee</u>-noh <u>teen</u>-toh/<u>blahn</u>-koh

lemonade/orangeade.   *limonada/naranjada.*
lee-moh-**nah**-dah/nah-rahn-**hah**-dah

a soft drink.   *un refresco.*   oon reh-**fress**-koh

376. What soft drinks do you have? (for.)
     ¿Qué refrescos tiene?   Keh reh-**fress**-kohss tee-**eh**-neh

377. Can you bring me a diet soda? (for.)
     ¿Me puede traer un refresco dietético?
     Meh **pweh**-deh trah-**ehr** **oon** reh-**fress**-koh dee-eh-**teh**-tee-koh

378. For dessert, bring me rice pudding. (for.)
     De postre, tráigame arroz con leche.
     Deh **pohss**-treh, **tri**-gah-meh ah-**rohss** kohn **leh**-cheh

     peaches in syrup.   *duraznos/melocotones en almíbar.*
     doo-**rahss**-nohss/meh-loh-koh-**toh**-ness en ahl-**mee**-bar

     caramel custard.   *flan.*   **flahn**

     strawberries and cream.   *fresas con crema/nata. (Sp.)*
     freh-sahss kohn **kreh**-mah/**nah**-tah

379. I would like to order some (vanilla/strawberry/chocolate)
     ice cream.
     Me gustaría ordenar un helado (de vainilla/fresa/chocolate).
     Meh goos-tah-**ree**-ah or-deh-**nar** el-**ah**-doh (deh vi-**nee**-yah/
     freh-sah/cho-koh-**lah**-teh)

     (lemon/mango/passion fruit) sherbet.
     nieve (de limón/mango/maracuyá). (Mex.)
     nee-**eh**-veh (deh lee-**mohn**/**mahn**-goh/mah-rah-koo-**yah**)

     (lemon/raspberry) sherbet.
     sorbete (de limón/frambuesa). (Sp.)
     sor-**beh**-teh (deh lee-**mohn**/frahm-**bweh**-sah)

     (three-milk) cake.   *pastel (de tres leches). (Mex.)*
     pahss-**tel** (deh trehss **leh**-chess)

     (cheese) cake.   *tarta (de queso). (Sp.)*
     tar-tah (deh **keh**-soh)

     (chocolate) cake.   *torta (de chocolate). (S. Am.)*
     tor-tah (deh choh-koh-**lah**-teh)

380. Would you like some coffee?   *¿Les gustaría un café?*
     Less goos-tah-**ree**-ah oon kah-**feh**

plain coffee. *café americano.*
kah-feh ah-meh-ree-kah-noh

coffee with spices and raw sugar.
café de olla. (Mex.) **kah-feh deh oh-yah**

espresso (with a dash of milk). *expreso (cortado).*
eks-press-oh (kor-tah-doh)

381. This needs a little salt/pepper/sugar.
Esto necesita un poco de sal/pimienta/azúcar.
**Ess-toh neh-seh-see-tah oon poh-koh deh sahl/pee-mee-en-tah/
ah-soo-kar**

382. This is delicious/disgusting.
Esto está delicioso/asqueroso.
Ess-toh ess-tah deh-lee-see-ohss-oh/ahss-keh-rohss-oh

383. Where is the bathroom?
¿Dónde está el baño/los servicios? (Sp.)
Dohn-deh ess-tah el bah-nyoh/lohss sehr-vee-see-ohss

the men's room? *el baño/los servicios para caballeros?*
el bah-nyoh/lohss sehr-vee-see-ohss pah-rah kah-bah-yeh-rohss

the ladies' room? *el baño/los servicios para damas?*
el bah-nyoh/lohss sehr-vee-see-ohss pah-rah dah-mahss

384. The check, please. *La cuenta, por favor.*
Lah kwen-tah por fah-vor

385. Is service/the tip included?
¿Está incluido el servicio/la propina?
Ess-tah een-kloo-ee-doh el sehr-vee-see-oh/lah proh-pee-nah

386. The check is wrong. *La cuenta está equivocada.*
Lah kwen-tah ess-tah eh-kee-voh-kah-dah

387. We did not order this. *No pedimos esto.*
Noh peh-dee-mohss ess-toh

388. I want to speak with the manager.
Quiero hablar con el gerente.
Kee-eh-roh ah-blar kohn el heh-ren-teh

KEEPING IN TOUCH

389. I need to make a phone call.
Necesito hacer una llamada telefónica.
Neh-seh-<u>see</u>-toh ah-<u>sehr</u> <u>oo</u>-nah yah-<u>mah</u>-dah
teh-leh-<u>foh</u>-nee-kah

an international call. *una llamada internacional.*
<u>oo</u>-nah yah-<u>mah</u>-dah een-tehr-nah-see-oh-<u>nahl</u>

a collect call. *una llamada por cobrar.*
<u>oo</u>-nah yah-<u>mah</u>-dah por koh-<u>brar</u>

390. Where can I connect to the Internet?
¿Dónde puedo conectarme a la red?
<u>Dohn</u>-deh <u>pweh</u>-doh koh-nek-<u>tar</u>-meh ah lah red

391. I have my own laptop computer.
Tengo mi propia computadora portátil.
<u>Ten</u>-goh mee <u>proh</u>-pee-ah kohm-poo-tah-<u>doh</u>-rah por-<u>tah</u>-teel

laptop computer. *propio ordenador portátil. (Sp.)*
<u>proh</u>-pree-oh or-deh-nah-<u>dor</u> por-<u>tah</u>-teel

392. Is there (free) Wi-Fi access here?
¿Hay acceso inalámbrico (gratis) aquí?
I ahk-<u>seh</u>-soh een-ahl-<u>ahm</u>-bree-koh (-<u>grah</u>-tees) ah-<u>kee</u>

393. I want to send an e-mail. *Quiero enviar/mandar un correo electrónico.* Kee-<u>eh</u>-roh en-vee-<u>ar</u>/mahn-<u>dar</u> oon koh-<u>reh</u>-oh eh-lek-<u>troh</u>-nee-koh

a text message. *un mensaje de texto.*
oon men-<u>sah</u>-heh deh <u>tex</u>-toh

a fax. *un fax.* oon fax

a letter (by air mail). *una carta (por correo aéreo).*
<u>oo</u>-nah <u>kar</u>-tah (por koh-<u>reh</u>-oh ah-<u>eh</u>-reh-oh)

a registered letter. *una carta certificada.*
<u>oo</u>-nah <u>kar</u>-tah sehr-tee-fee-<u>kah</u>-dah

an express letter. *una carta urgente.*
<u>oo</u>-nah <u>kar</u>-tah oor-<u>hen</u>-teh

a postcard. *una postal.* <u>oo</u>-nah pohss-<u>tahl</u>

a package (overnight). *un paquete (para el día siguiente).*
oon pah-<u>keh</u>-teh (-<u>pah</u>-rah el <u>dee</u>-ah see-gee-<u>en</u>-teh)

394. Careful! It's fragile.   *¡Cuidado! Es frágil.*
Kwee-**dah**-doh ess **frah**-heel

395. Where is the post office?   *¿Dónde está la oficina de correos?*
Dohn-deh ess-**tah** lah oh-fee-**see**-nah deh koh-**reh**-ohss
the mail box?   *el buzón?*   el boo-**sohn**

396. I would like to buy a calling card.
Quisiera comprar una tarjeta telefónica.
Kee-see-**eh**-rah kohm-**prar** **oo**-nah tar-**heh**-tah
teh-leh-**foh**-nee-kah
a pre-paid cell phone.   *un teléfono celular/móvil pre-pagado.*
oon teh-**leh**-foh-noh seh-loo-**lar**/**moh**-veel preh-pah-**gah**-doh
a SIM card.   *una tarjeta SIM.*   **oo**-nah tar-**heh**-tah seem

397. There's no signal.   *No hay señal.*   Noh I seh-**nyahl**

398. We must be outside the service area.
Debemos estar fuera del área de servicio.
Deh-**beh**-mohss ess-**tahr** **fweh**-rah del **ah**-reh-ah deh
sehr-**vee**-see-oh

399. What's your e-mail address?
¿Cuál es tu dirección de correo electrónico?
Kwahl ess too dee-rek-see-**ohn** deh koh-**reh**-oh
eh-lek-**troh**-nee-koh
your (cell) phone number?
tu número de teléfono (celular/móvil)?
too **noo**-mehr-oh deh teh-**leh**-foh-noh (-seh-loo-**lar**/**moh**-veel)

400. My e-mail address is . . .
Mi dirección de correo electrónico es . . .
Mee dee-rek-see-**ohn** deh koh-**reh**-oh eh-lek-**troh**-nee-koh ess

401. My (cell) phone number is . . .
Mi número de teléfono (celular/móvil) es . . .
Mee **noo**-meh-roh deh teh-**leh**-foh-noh (seh-loo-**lar**/**moh**-veel) ess

402. Call me.   *Llámame.*   **Yah**-mah-meh

403. It's (always) busy.   *(Siempre) Está ocupado.*
(See-**em**-preh) Ess-**tah** oh-koo-**pah**-doh

404. There's a lot of interference.   *Hay mucha interferencia.*
     I <u>moo</u>-chah een-tehr-feh-<u>ren</u>-see-ah

405. I can't hear you. (inf.)   *No te escucho.*
     Noh teh ess-<u>koo</u>-choh

406. Speak louder. (inf.)   *Habla más fuerte.*
     <u>Ah</u>-blah mahss <u>fwehr</u>-teh

407. The call was cut off.   *Se cortó la llamada.*
     Seh kor-<u>toh</u> lah yah-<u>mah</u>-dah

408. Wrong number.   *El número está equivocado.*
     El <u>noo</u>-meh-roh ess-<u>tah</u> eh-kee-voh-<u>kah</u>-doh

409. Who's speaking?   *¿Quién habla?*   Kee-<u>en</u> <u>ah</u>-blah

410. May I speak to . . . ?   *¿Puedo hablar con . . . ?*
     <u>Pweh</u>-doh ah-<u>blar</u> kohn

411. Do you know at what time he/she'll be back? (for.)
     ¿Sabe a qué hora vuelve?
     -<u>Sah</u>-beh ah keh <u>oh</u>-rah <u>vwel</u>-veh

412. Please tell him/her I called. (for.)
     Por favor dígale que llamé.
     Por fah-<u>vor</u> <u>dee</u>-gah-leh keh yah-<u>meh</u>

413. He/she has my number.   *Él/ella tiene mi número.*
     El/<u>Eh</u>-yah tee-<u>eh</u>-neh mee <u>noo</u>-meh-roh

414. I will call later.   *Llamaré más tarde.*
     Yah-mah-<u>reh</u> mahss <u>tar</u>-deh

415. It's (not) (very) important.   *(No) es (muy) importante.*
     (Noh) ess (mooy) eem-por-<u>tahn</u>-teh

416. I tried calling you several times. (inf.)
     Traté de llamarte varias veces.
     Trah-<u>teh</u> deh yah-<u>mar</u>-teh <u>vah</u>-ree-ahss <u>veh</u>-sess

417. Where were you? (inf.)   *¿Dónde estabas?*
     <u>Dohn</u>-deh ess-<u>tah</u>-bahss

418. Did you get my message? (inf.)
     ¿Recibiste mi recado?   Reh-see-<u>bees</u>-teh mee reh-<u>kah</u>-doh

419. Do you have a phone book? (for.)
¿Tiene un directorio telefónico?
Tee-**eh**-neh oon dee-rek-**toh**-ree-oh teh-leh-**foh**-nee-koh

the yellow pages? *la sección amarilla?*
lah sek-see-**ohn** ah-mah-**ree**-yah

420. I need to look up a number/an address.
Necesito buscar un número/una dirección.
Neh-seh-**see**-toh boos-**kahr** oon **noo**-meh-roh/**oo**-nah
dee-rek-see-**ohn**

421. I'm looking for an Internet café (with Macs).
Estoy buscando un cibercafé (con Macs).
Ess-**toy** boos-**kahn**-doh oon see-behr-kah-**feh** (kohn Macs)

a public phone. *un teléfono público.*
oon teh-**leh**-foh-noh **poo**-blee-koh

422. What's the rate per minute? *¿Cuál es la tarifa por minuto?*
Kwahl ess lah tah-**ree**-fah por mee-**noo**-toh

423. Can I print a document? *¿Puedo imprimir un documento?*
Pweh-doh eem-pree-**meer** oon doh-koo-**men**-toh

424. How do I scan these pages? *¿Cómo escaneo estas páginas?*
Koh-moh ess-kah-**neh**-oh **ess**-tahss **pah**-hee-nahss

425. Help me make a photocopy. (for.)
Ayúdeme a hacer una fotocopia.
Ah-**yoo**-deh-meh ah ah-**sehr** **oo**-nah foh-toh-**koh**-pee-ah

426. How much is it per page? *¿Cuánto cuesta por página?*
Kwahn-toh **kwess**-tah por **pah**-hee-nah

RELIGIOUS SERVICES

427. I'm an atheist. *Soy ateo.* Soy ah-**teh**-oh
Ba'hai. *ba'hai.* **bah**-hai
Buddhist. *budista.* boo-**dees**-tah
Catholic. *católico.* kah-**toh**-lee-koh
Christian. *cristiano.* krees-tee-**ah**-noh
Jewish. *judío.* hoo-**dee**-oh
Muslim. *Musulmán.* moo-sool-**mahn**

428. Where is the church?   *¿Dónde está la iglesia?*
Dohn-deh ess-**tah** lah ee-**gleh**-see-ah

the mosque?   *la mezquita?*   lah mess-**kee**-tah

the synagogue?   *la sinagoga?*   lah see-nah-**goh**-gah

the temple?   *el templo?*   el **tem**-ploh

429. At what time are services held?
¿A qué hora son los servicios?
Ah keh **oh**-rah sohn lohss sehr-**vee**-see-ohss

CULTURE & ENTERTAINMENT

430. Let's go to the (contemporary) art museum.
Vamos al museo de arte (contemporáneo).
Vah-mohss ahl moo-**seh**-oh deh **ar**-teh
kohn-tem-por-**ah**-neh-oh

archaeology museum.   *museo de arqueología.*
moo-**seh**-oh deh ar-keh-oh-loh-**gee**-ah

the craft museum.   *museo de artesanías.*
moo-**seh**-oh deh ar-teh-sah-**nee**-ahss

the natural history museum.   *museo de historia natural.*
moo-**seh**-oh deh ees-**toh**-ree-ah nah-too-**rahl**

431. At what time does it open/close?   *¿A qué hora abre/cierra?*
Ah keh **oh**-rah **ah**-breh/see-**eh**-rah

432. Is there a discount for students/teachers?
¿Hay descuento para estudiantes/profesores?
I des-**kwen**-toh **pah**-rah ess-too-dee-**ahn**-tess/proh-feh-**soh**-ress

for children?   *para niños?*   **pah**-rah **nee**-nyohss

for the elderly?   *para ancianos?*   **pah**-rah ahn-see-**ah**-nohss

433. Is it handicap-accessible?
¿Hay acceso para minusválidos?
I ahk-**seh**-soh **pah**-rah mee-noos-**vahl**-ee-dohss

434. I'm interested in the painting exhibition.
Me interesa la exposición de pintura.
Meh een-tehr-**eh**-sah lah eks-poh-see-see-**ohn** deh peen-**too**-rah

the sculpture exhibition.   *la exposición de escultura.*
lah eks-poh-see-see-<u>ohn</u> deh ess-kool-<u>too</u>-rah

the pre-Hispanic art exhibition.
la exposición de arte prehispánico.
lah eks-poh-see-see-<u>ohn</u> deh <u>ar</u>-teh preh-ees-<u>pah</u>-nee-koh

435. We want to take a guided tour of the museum.
Queremos una visita guiada del museo.
Keh-<u>reh</u>-mohss <u>oo</u>-nah vee-<u>see</u>-tah gee-<u>ah</u>-dah del moo-<u>seh</u>-oh

of the city.   *de la ciudad.*   deh lah <u>see</u>-oo-dahd

436. Is (flash) photography allowed?
¿Se permite tomar fotografías (con flash)?
Seh pehr-<u>mee</u>-teh toh-<u>mar</u> foh-toh-grah-<u>fee</u>-ahss (kohn flash)

437. Don't you all want to go to the movies?
¿No quieren ir al cine?
Noh kee-<u>eh</u>-ren eer ahl <u>see</u>-neh

438. Which direction is the theatre?
¿Hacia dónde está el teatro?
Ah-<u>see</u>-yah <u>dohn</u>-deh ess-<u>tah</u> el teh-<u>ah</u>-troh

439. What's playing?   *¿Qué hay en la cartelera?*
Keh I en lah kar-teh-<u>leh</u>-rah

440. At what time is the show?   *¿A qué hora es la función?*
Ah keh <u>oh</u>-rah ess lah foon-see-<u>ohn</u>

441. How much are the tickets?
¿Cuánto cuestan los boletos/las entradas?
<u>Kwahn</u>-toh <u>kwess</u>-tahn lohss boh-<u>leh</u>-tohss/lahss en-<u>trah</u>-dahss

442. Is the movie dubbed in Spanish?
¿Está doblada al español la película?
Ess-<u>tah</u> doh-<u>blah</u>-dah ahl ess-pah-<u>nyohl</u> lah peh-<u>lee</u>-koo-lah

443. Did you like the movie/the play?
¿Te gustó la película/la obra?
Teh goos-<u>toh</u> lah peh-<u>lee</u>-koo-lah/lah <u>oh</u>-brah

444. I liked it (a lot).   *Me gustó (mucho).*
Meh goos-<u>toh</u> (<u>moo</u>-choh)

445. I didn't like it (at all).   *No me gustó (nada).*
      Noh meh goos-<u>toh</u> (<u>nah</u>-dah)

446. What's your favorite movie?   *¿Cuál es tu película favorita?*
      Kwahl ess too peh-<u>lee</u>-koo-lah fah-voh-<u>ree</u>-tah

447. Do you like to dance? (inf.)   *¿Te gusta bailar?*
      Teh <u>goos</u>-tah bi-<u>lar</u>

448. Can we go to a (rock/classical music) concert?
      ¿Podemos ir a un concierto (de rock/música clásica)?
      Poh-<u>deh</u>-mohss eer ah oon kohn-see-<u>ehr</u>-toh (de rock/<u>moo</u>-see-kah <u>klahss</u>-see-kah)

      to a fun place?   *ir a un lugar divertido?*
      eer ah oon loo-<u>gar</u> dee-vehr-<u>tee</u>-doh

      to a nightclub?   *ir a un club nocturno/una discoteca?*
      eer ah oon kloob nohk-<u>toor</u>-noh/<u>oo</u>-nah dees-koh-<u>teh</u>-kah

      to a gay bar?   *ir a un bar gay?*   eer ah oon bar gay

449. What's the cover charge?   *¿Cuánto cuesta la entrada?*
      <u>Kwahn</u>-toh <u>kwess</u>-tah lah en-<u>trah</u>-dah

450. Do I need to take an ID?
      ¿Necesito llevar una identificación?
      Neh-seh-<u>see</u>-toh yeh-<u>vahr</u> <u>oo</u>-nah ee-den-tee-fee-kah-see-<u>ohn</u>

451. I'm over eighteen years old.   *Soy mayor de dieciocho años.*
      Soy mah-<u>yor</u> deh dee-eh-see-<u>oh</u>-choh <u>ah</u>-nyohss.

452. I (don't) drink alcohol.   *(No) Bebo alcohol.*
      (Noh) <u>Beh</u>-boh ahl-<u>kohl</u>

453. I (don't) like drugs.   *(No)Me gustan las drogas.*
      (Noh) Meh <u>goos</u>-tahn lahss <u>droh</u>-gahss

454. We are (not) going out tonight.
      (No) Vamos a salir esta noche.
      (Noh) <u>Vah</u>-mohss ah sah-<u>leer</u> <u>ess</u>-tah <u>noh</u>-cheh

455. We have other plans this weekend.
      Tenemos otros planes este fin de semana.
      Teh-<u>neh</u>-mohss <u>oh</u>-trohss <u>plah</u>-nehss <u>ess</u>-teh feen deh seh-<u>mah</u>-nah

456. Do you want to go with me? (inf.)   *¿Quieres ir conmigo?*
    Kee-<u>eh</u>-ress eer kohn-<u>mee</u>-goh

457. Would you like to dance with me? (inf.)
    ¿Quieres bailar conmigo?   Kee-<u>eh</u>-ress bi-<u>lar</u> kohn-<u>mee</u>-goh

458. At what time shall we meet?   *¿A qué hora nos vemos?*
    Ah keh <u>oh</u>-rah nohss <u>veh</u>-mohss

459. Where shall we meet?   *¿Dónde nos vemos?*
    <u>Dohn</u>-deh nohss <u>veh</u>-mohss

460. We will meet at the entrance.   *Nos vemos en la entrada.*
    Nohss <u>veh</u>-mohss en lah en-<u>trah</u>-dah

461. Can you pick us up? (inf.)   *¿Puedes pasar a recogernos?*
    <u>Pweh</u>-dess pah-<u>sar</u> ah reh-koh-<u>hehr</u>-nohss

462. This is fun/boring.   *Esto está muy divertido/aburrido.*
    <u>Ess</u>-toh ess-<u>tah</u> mooy dee-vehr-<u>tee</u>-doh/ah-boo-<u>ree</u>-doh

463. Let's go somewhere else.   *Vamos a otro lado.*
    <u>Vah</u>-mohss ah <u>oh</u>-troh <u>lah</u>-doh

MONEY & SHOPPING

464. I need to change currencies.   *Necesito cambiar dinero.*
    Neh-seh-<u>see</u>-toh kahm-bee-<u>ar</u> dee-<u>neh</u>-roh

465. I have to buy some traveler's checks.
    Tengo que comprar unos cheques de viajero.
    <u>Ten</u>-goh keh kohm-<u>prar</u> <u>oo</u>-nohss <u>cheh</u>-kess deh
    vee-ah-<u>heh</u>-roh

466. Where is there a bank?   *¿Dónde hay un banco?*
    <u>Dohn</u>-deh I oon <u>bahn</u>-koh

467. Is there a currency exchange office around here?
    ¿Hay una casa de cambio por aquí?
    I <u>oo</u>-nah <u>kah</u>-sah deh <u>kahm</u>-bee-oh por ah-<u>kee</u>

468. What's the exchange rate?   *¿Cuál es el tipo de cambio?*
    Kwahl ess el <u>tee</u>-poh deh <u>kahm</u>-bee-oh

469. Do I have to pay a commission?
    ¿Hay que pagar una comisión?
    I keh pah-<u>gar</u> <u>oo</u>-nah koh-mee-see-<u>ohn</u>

470.   Give me small bills, please. (for.)
Deme billetes pequeños, por favor.
Deh-meh bee-yeh-tess peh-keh-nyohss, por fah-vor

471.   Can you give me a receipt?   *¿Me puede dar un recibo?*
Meh pweh-deh dar oon reh-see-boh

472.   Let's go to an ATM.   *Vamos a un cajero automático.*
Vah-mohss ah oon kah-heh-roh ow-toh-mah-tee-koh

473.   We (don't) have a lot of money.
(No) Tenemos (mucho) dinero.
(Noh) Teh-neh-mohss moo-choh dee-neh-roh

474.   We (don't) want to spend a lot.   *(No) Queremos gastar mucho.*
(Noh) Keh-reh-mohss gahss-tahr moo-choh

475.   I want to go to a clothing store.
Quiero ir a una tienda de ropa.
Kee-eh-roh eer ah oo-nah tee-en-dah deh roh-pah

shoe store.   *una tienda de zapatos/zapatería.*
oo-nah tee-en-dah deh sah-pah-tohss/sah-pah-teh-ree-ah

a handicrafts store.   *una tienda de artesanías.*
oo-nah tee-en-dah deh ar-teh-sah-nee-ahss

a traditional market.   *a un mercado típico.*
ah oon mehr-kah-doh tee-pee-koh

a shopping mall.   *un centro comercial.*
oon sen-troh koh-mehr-see-ahl

a jewelry store.   *una joyería.*   oo-nah hoy-eh-ree-ah

476.   Do you know where I can find a (used, English) book store?
*¿Sabe dónde puedo encontrar una librería
(de libros usados, en inglés)?*
Sah-beh dohn-deh pweh-doh en-kohn-trar oo-nah lee-breh-ree-ah (deh lee-brohss oo-sah-dohss, en-een-gless)

an office-supply store?   *una papelería?*
oo-nah pah-pel-eh-ree-ah

a hardware store?   *una ferretería?*
oo-nah fehr-reh-teh-ree-ah

477.   Where can I buy souvenirs?
¿Dónde puedo comprar recuerdos?
Dohn-deh pweh-doh kohm-prar reh-kwehr-dohss

478. (Where) Can I try this on?   ¿(Dónde) Puedo probarme esto?
(**Dohn**-deh) **Pweh**-doh proh-**bar**-meh **ess**-toh

479. I need a bigger/smaller size.
Necesito una talla más grande/chica.
Neh-seh-**see**-toh **oo**-nah **tah**-yah mahss **grahn**-deh/**chee**-kah

480. Do you have other colors/models?
¿Tiene otros colores/modelos?
Tee-**eh**-neh **oh**-trohss koh-**loh**-ress/moh-**deh**-lohss

a mirror?   *un espejo?*   oon ess-**peh**-hoh

481. How much does this cost?   ¿Cuánto cuesta/vale esto?
Kwahn-toh **kwess**-tah/**vah**-leh **ess**-toh

482. What's the price of that?   ¿Qué precio tiene eso?
Keh **preh**-see-oh tee-**en**-eh **eh**-soh

483. It's very expensive/cheap.   *Es muy caro/barato.*
Ess mooy **kah**-roh/bah-**rah**-toh

484. It's too much.   *Es demasiado.*   Ess deh-mah-see-**ah**-doh

485. Can you give me a good/better price? (for.)
¿Me puede dar un buen/mejor precio?
Meh **pweh**-deh dar oon bwen/meh-**hor** **preh**-see-oh

486. I can't pay so much.   *No puedo pagar tanto.*
Noh **pweh**-doh pah-**gar** **tahn**-toh

487. I don't have enough money.   *No me alcanza el dinero.*
Noh meh ahl-**kahn**-sah el dee-**neh**-roh

488. It has a twenty percent discount.
Tiene un descuento del veinte por ciento.
Tee-**eh**-neh oon dess-**kwen**-toh del **vayn**-teh por see-**en**-toh

489. It's on sale.   *Está de rebaja.*   Ess-**tah** deh reh-**bah**-hah

490. I'll take it.   *Me lo llevo.*   Meh loh **yeh**-voh

491. Does it have a warranty?   ¿Tiene garantía?
Tee-**eh**-neh gah-rahn-**tee**-ah

492. Where do I pay?   ¿Dónde se paga?
Dohn-deh seh **pah**-gah

493. Do you accept credit cards? *¿Aceptan tarjetas de crédito?*
Ah-<u>sep</u>-tahn tar-<u>heh</u>-tahss deh <u>kreh</u>-dee-toh

debit cards? *tarjetas de débito?*
tar-<u>heh</u>-tahss deh <u>deh</u>-bee-toh

American dollars? *dólares americanos?*
<u>doh</u>-lah-ress ah-meh-ree-<u>kah</u>-nohss

494. Can I return it? *¿Puedo devolverlo?*
<u>Pweh</u>-doh deh-vohl-<u>vehr</u>-loh

495. I need a receipt. *Necesito un recibo.*
Neh-seh-<u>see</u>-toh oon reh-<u>see</u>-boh

496. Can you (gift) wrap it? (for.)
¿Lo puede envolver (para regalo)?
Loh <u>pweh</u>-deh en-vohl-<u>vehr</u> (<u>pah</u>-rah reh-<u>gah</u>-loh)

497. Can you put it in a bag/box?
¿Lo puede poner en una bolsa/caja?
Loh <u>pweh</u>-deh poh-<u>nehr</u> en <u>oo</u>-nah <u>bol</u>-sah/<u>kah</u>-hah

498. I believe it's defective. *Creo que está defectuoso.*
<u>Kreh</u>-oh keh ess-<u>tah</u> deh-fek-<u>twoh</u>-soh

499. It doesn't work. *No funciona.* **Noh foon-see-<u>oh</u>-nah**

500. I want to return it. *Quiero devolverlo.*
Kee-<u>eh</u>-roh deh-vohl-<u>vehr</u>-loh

501. I need a replacement. *Necesito una substitución.*
Neh-seh-<u>see</u>-toh <u>oo</u>-nah soob-stee-too-see-<u>ohn</u>

502. Please give me a refund. *Por favor deme un reembolso.*
Por fah-<u>vor</u> deh-meh oon ray-em-<u>bol</u>-soh

COMPUTERS & INTERNET

503. I need to use a computer. *Necesito usar una computadora.*
Neh-seh-<u>see</u>-toh oo-<u>sar</u> <u>oo</u>-nah kohm-poo-tah-<u>doh</u>-rah

a computer. *un ordenador. (Sp.)* oon or-deh-nah-<u>dor</u>

504. Where can I connect to the Internet?
¿Dónde puedo conectarme a la red?
<u>Dohn</u>-deh <u>pweh</u>-doh koh-nek-<u>tar</u>-meh ah lah red?

505. Do you have a laptop computer? (inf.)
¿Tienes una computadora portátil?
Tee-<u>eh</u>-ness <u>oo</u>-nah kohm-poo-tah-<u>doh</u>-rah por-<u>tah</u>-teel

a laptop computer?   *un ordenador portátil? (Sp.)*
oon or-deh-nah-<u>dor</u> por-<u>tah</u>-teel

506. Is it a Mac or a PC?   *¿Es una Mac o una PC?*
Ess <u>oo</u>-nah Mac oh <u>oo</u>-nah peh-<u>seh</u>

507. I don't know the keyboard shortcuts.
No conozco los atajos del teclado.
Noh koh-<u>nohss</u>-koh lohss ah-<u>tah</u>-hohss del teh-<u>klah</u>-doh

508. How can I get on-line?   *¿Cómo puedo conectarme a la red?*
<u>Koh</u>-moh <u>pweh</u>-doh koh-nek-<u>tar</u>-meh ah lah red

get off-line?   *desconectarme de la red?*
dess-koh-nek-<u>tar</u>-meh deh lah red

509. I would like to check my e-mail.
Quisiera revisar mi correo electrónico.
Kee-see-<u>eh</u>-rah reh-vee-<u>sar</u> mee koh-<u>reh</u>-oh eh-lek-<u>troh</u>-nee-koh

send an e-mail.   *enviar/mandar un correo electrónico.*
en-vee-<u>ahr</u>/mahn-<u>dar</u> oon koh-<u>reh</u>-oh eh-lek-<u>troh</u>-nee-koh

510. My e-mail address is . . .   *Mi dirección electrónica es . . .*
Mee dee-rek-see-<u>ohn</u> eh-lek-<u>troh</u>-nee-kah ess

511. It's iluvspanish@[at] mymail.[dot] com.
Es iluvspanish@ [arroba] mymail.[punto] com.
Ess iluvspanish ah-<u>roh</u>-bah mymail <u>poon</u>-toh com

512. What's the name of the website?
¿Cómo se llama el sitio electrónico?
<u>Koh</u>-moh seh <u>yah</u>-mah el <u>see</u>-tee-oh eh-lek-<u>troh</u>-nee-koh

513. First, open the browser. (inf.)
Primero, abre el navegador.
Pree-<u>meh</u>-roh <u>ah</u>-breh el nah-veh-gah-<u>dohr</u>

514. You can use the desktop shortcut. (inf.)
Puedes usar el acceso directo en el escritorio.
<u>Pweh</u>-dess oo-<u>sar</u> el ahk-<u>seh</u>-soh dee-<u>rek</u>-toh en el ess-kree-<u>toh</u>-ree-oh

515. Search for the webpage. (inf.)   *Busca la página electrónica.*
Boos-kah lah pah-hee-nah eh-lek-troh-nee-kah

516. What's your favorite search engine? (inf.)
¿Cuál es tu buscador favorito?
Kwahl ess too boos-kah-dohr fah-voh-ree-toh

517. I want to go to the site's home page.
Quiero ir a la página principal del sitio.
Kee-eh-roh eer ah lah pah-hee-nah preen-see-pahl del
see-tee-oh

518. Click on the link. (inf.)   *Haz clic en el enlace.*
Ahss kleek en el en-lah-seh

519. My username is . . .   *Mi nombre de usuario es . . .*
Mee nohm-breh deh oo-swah-ree-oh ess

520. What's the password?   *¿Cuál es la contraseña?*
Kwahl ess lah kohn-trah-seh-nyah

521. I have too much spam/junk mail.
Tengo demasiado correo basura.
Ten-goh deh-mah-see-ah-doh koh-reh-oh bah-soo-rah

522. I want to edit the message.   *Quiero editar el mensaje.*
Kee-eh-roh eh-dee-tar el men-sah-heh

copy and paste this word.   *copiar y pegar esta palabra.*
koh-pee-ar ee peh-gar ess-tah pah-lah-brah

cut and paste these lines.   *cortar y pegar estas líneas.*
kor-tar ee peh-gar ess-tahss lee-neh-ahss

delete this section.   *borrar esta sección.*
boh-rar ess-tah sek-see-ohn

523. I need to save the document to the hard disk.
Necesito guardar el documento en el disco duro.
Neh-seh-see-toh gwar-dar el doh-koo-men-toh en el dees-koh
doo-roh

save it in a new folder.   *guardarlo en una carpeta nueva.*
gwar-dar-loh en oo-nah kar-peh-tah nweh-vah

save it as a PDF.   *guardarlo como un PDF.*
gwar-dar-loh koh-moh oon peh deh eh-feh

524. Is it possible to print it from here?
¿Es posible imprimirlo desde aquí?
Ess poh-<u>see</u>-bleh eem-pree-<u>meer</u>-loh <u>dess</u>-deh ah-<u>kee</u>

525. The printer is running out of ink/toner.
Se le está acabando la tinta/el toner a la impresora.
Seh leh ess-<u>tah</u> ah-kah-<u>bahn</u>-doh lah <u>teen</u>-tah/el toh-<u>nehr</u> ah lah eem-preh-<u>soh</u>-rah

526. The paper jammed.   *Se atoró el papel.*
Seh ah-toh-<u>roh</u> el pah-<u>pel</u>

527. I'm missing some pages.   *Me faltan algunas páginas.*
Meh <u>fahl</u>-tahn ahl-<u>goo</u>-nahss <u>pah</u>-hee-nahss

528. Can I attach a file?   *¿Puedo adjuntar un archivo?*
<u>Pweh</u>-doh ahd-hoon-<u>tar</u> oon ahr-<u>chee</u>-voh

529. How do I open the attached file?
¿Cómo abro el archivo adjunto?
<u>Koh</u>-moh <u>ah</u>-broh el ahr-<u>chee</u>-voh ahd-<u>hoon</u>-toh

 save the attached file?   *guardo el archivo adjunto?*
<u>gwar</u>-doh el ahr-<u>chee</u>-voh ad-<u>hoon</u>-toh

530. Just drag it and drop it. (inf.)   *Sólo arrástralo y colócalo.*
<u>Soh</u>-loh ah-<u>rahss</u>-trah-loh ee koh-<u>loh</u>-kah-loh

531. Does this computer have antivirus software?
¿Tiene un programa antivirus esta computadora?
Tee-<u>eh</u>-neh oon proh-<u>grah</u>-mah ahn-tee-<u>vee</u>-roos <u>ess</u>-tah kohm-poo-tah-<u>doh</u>-rah

532. Did you remember to back up your work? (inf.)
¿Te acordaste de respaldar tu trabajo?
Teh ah-kor-<u>dahss</u>-teh deh ress-pahl-<u>dahr</u> too trah-<u>bah</u>-hoh

533. Don't forget to turn off the equipment. (inf.)
No olvides apagar el equipo.
Noh ohl-<u>vee</u>-dess ah-pah-<u>gar</u> el eh-<u>kee</u>-poh

BUSINESS TRAVEL

534. I came for a conference.   *Vine a una conferencia.*
<u>Vee</u>-neh ah <u>oo</u>-nah kohn-feh-<u>ren</u>-see-ah

535. I'm taking a (Spanish) course.
      Estoy tomando un curso (de español).
      Ess-**toy** toh-**mahn**-doh oon **koor**-soh (deh ess-pah-**nyohl**)

536. I'm here on official business.
      Estoy aquí por asuntos oficiales.
      Ess-**toy** ah-**kee** por ahss-**soon**-tohss oh-fee-see-**ah**-less

537. The meeting is at eleven sharp.
      La junta es a las once en punto.
      Lah **hoon**-tah es ah lahss **ohn**-seh en **poon**-toh

538. I don't want to be late.
      No quiero llegar tarde.
      Noh kee-**eh**-roh yeh-**gar** **tar**-deh

539. I'm late, forgive me. (for.)   *Estoy retrasado, disculpe.*
      Ess-**toy** reh-trah-**sah**-doh, dees-**kool**-peh

540. I have an appointment with the President.
      Tengo una cita con el presidente.
      Ten-goh **oo**-nah **see**-tah kohn el preh-see-**den**-teh

      the Vice-President (for Sales).   *el vicepresidente (de ventas).*
      el vee-seh-preh-see-**den**-teh (deh **ven**-tahss)

541. Where is his/her office?   *¿Dónde está su oficina?*
      Dohn-deh ess-**tah** soo oh-fee-**see**-nah

      the elevator?   *el elevador/ascensor?*
      el eh-leh-vah-**dor**/ah-sen-**sor**

542. I (don't) need an interpreter.   *(No) Necesito un intérprete.*
      (Noh) Neh-seh-**see**-toh oon een-**tehr**-preh-teh

543. Do you have a business card? (for.)   *¿Tiene una tarjeta?*
      Tee-**eh**-neh **oo**-nah tar-**heh**-tah

544. Here is my card.   *Aquí está mi tarjeta.*
      Ah-**kee** ess-**tah** mee tar-**heh**-tah

545. I need to call headquarters.
      Necesito llamar a la oficina central.
      Neh-seh-**see**-toh yah-**mar** ah lah oh-fee-**see**-nah sen-**trahl**

      my boss.   *a mi jefe.*   ah mee **heh**-feh

      my spouse.   *a mi esposo/-a.*   ah mee ess-**poh**-soh/-ah

546. Can we sign the contract now?
¿Podemos firmar el contrato ahora?
Poh-<u>deh</u>-mohss feer-<u>mar</u> el kohn-<u>trah</u>-toh ah-<u>oh</u>-rah

547. We need more time to think it over.
Necesitamos más tiempo para pensarlo.
Neh-seh-see-<u>tah</u>-mohss mahss tee-<u>em</u>-poh
<u>pah</u>-rah- pen-<u>sahr</u>-loh

THE ENVIRONMENT

548. I'm concerned about the environment.
Me preocupa el medio ambiente.
Meh preh-oh-<u>koo</u>-pah el <u>meh</u>-dee-oh ahm-bee-<u>en</u>-teh

549. This city is very polluted.
Esta ciudad está muy contaminada.
<u>Ess</u>-tah <u>see</u>-oo-dahd ess-<u>tah</u> mooy kohn-tah-mee-<u>nah</u>-dah

550. There is too much trash.   *Hay demasiada basura.*
I deh-mah-see-<u>ah</u>-dah bah-<u>soo</u>-rah

551. Where is there a recycling center?
¿Dónde hay un centro de reciclaje?
<u>Dohn</u>-deh I oon <u>sen</u>-troh deh reh-see-<u>klah</u>-heh

552. Do you recycle paper/cardboard?   *¿Reciclan papel/cartón?*
Reh-<u>see</u>-klahn pah-<u>pel</u>/kar-<u>tohn</u>

plastics?   *plásticos?*   <u>plahss</u>-tee-kohss

glass?   *vidrio?*   <u>vee</u>-dree-oh

aluminum?   *aluminio?*   ah-loo-<u>mee</u>-nee-oh

553. Let's not waste water/food.   *No desperdiciemos agua/comida.*
Noh dess-pehr-dee-see-<u>eh</u>-mohss <u>ah</u>-wah/koh-<u>mee</u>-dah

554. Let's turn off the lights.   *Apaguemos las luces.*
Ah-pah-<u>geh</u>-mohss lahss <u>loo</u>-sess

555. Let's turn down the air conditioning.
Bajemos el aire acondicionado.
Bah-<u>heh</u>-mohss el <u>I</u>-reh ah-kohn-dee-see-oh-<u>nah</u>-doh

556. I want to buy organic products.
     Quiero comprar productos orgánicos.
     Kee-eh-roh kohm-prar proh-dook-tohss or-gah-nee-kohss

557. Where are local products sold?
     ¿Dónde se venden productos locales?
     Dohn-deh seh ven-den proh-dook-tohss loh-kah-less

558. What is locally produced?   *¿Qué se produce localmente?*
     Keh seh proh-doo-seh loh-kahl-men-teh

SPORTS & EXERCISE

559. I'm (not) in good shape.   *(No) Estoy en buena forma.*
     (Noh) Ess-toy en bweh-nah for-mah

560. I (don't) like to exercise.   *(No) Me gusta hacer ejercicio.*
     (Noh) Meh goos-tah ah-sehr eh-hehr-see-see-oh

561. I want to jog in the park.   *Quiero correr en el parque.*
     Kee-eh-roh koh-rehr en el par-keh

562. Can I walk around here?   *¿Puedo caminar por aquí?*
     Pweh-doh kah-mee-nar por ah-kee

563. I would like to go to the gym.   *Me gustaría ir al gimnasio.*
     Meh goos-tah-ree-ah eer ahl heem-nah-see-oh

     go swimming.   *ir a nadar.*   **eer ah nah-dar**

     ride a bike.   *andar en bicicleta.*   **ahn-dar en bee-see-kleh-tah**

564. What's your favorite sport?
     ¿Cuál es tu deporte favorito?
     Kwahl ess too deh-por-teh fah-voh-ree-toh

565. Is there a national sport?   *¿Hay un deporte nacional?*
     I oon deh-por-teh nah-see-oh-nahl

566. I prefer watching sports on TV.
     Prefiero ver los deportes en la televisión.
     **Preh-fee-eh-roh vehr lohss deh-por-tess en lah
     teh-leh-vee-see-ohn**

567. I lift weights.   *Levanto pesas.*   Leh-<u>vahn</u>-toh <u>peh</u>-sahss

568. I practice martial arts.   *Practico artes marciales.*
Prahk-<u>tee</u>-koh <u>ahr</u>-tess mar-see-<u>ah</u>-less

569. Have you tried yoga? (inf.)   *Has probado el yoga?*
Ahss proh-<u>bah</u>-doh el <u>yoh</u>-gah?

570. I do aerobics.   *Hago ejercicios aeróbicos.*
<u>Ah</u>-goh eh-hehr-<u>see</u>-see-ohss I-<u>roh</u>-bee-kohss

571. I really like playing golf.   *Me encanta jugar golf.*
Meh en-<u>kahn</u>-tah hoo-<u>gar</u> gohlf

tennis.   *tenis.*   -<u>teh</u>-nees

basketball.   *baloncesto.*   -bah-lohn-<u>sess</u>-toh

volleyball.   *voleibol.*   -voh-lay-<u>bohl</u>

572. Can we go to a soccer match?
¿Podemos ir a un partido de futbol?
Poh-<u>deh</u>-mohss eer ah oon par-<u>tee</u>-doh deh <u>foot</u>-bohl

573. What's the local team's name?
¿Cómo se llama el equipo local?
<u>Koh</u>-moh seh <u>yah</u>-mah el eh-<u>kee</u>-poh loh-<u>kahl</u>

574. Are you a (big) fan? (inf.)   *¿Eres un (gran) hincha?*
<u>Eh</u>-ress oon (grahn) <u>een</u>-chah

575. When is the bull-fighting season?
¿Cuándo es la temporada de toros?
<u>Kwahn</u>-doh ess lah tem-poh-<u>rah</u>-dah deh <u>toh</u>-rohss

576. Is boxing/wrestling popular?
¿Es popular el boxeo/la lucha libre?
Ess poh-poo-<u>lar</u> el bohk-<u>seh</u>-oh/lah <u>loo</u>-chah <u>lee</u>-breh

HEALTH & WELLNESS

577. I don't feel well.   *No me siento bien.*
Noh meh see-<u>en</u>-toh bee-<u>en</u>

578. I feel (very) ill.   *Me siento (muy) mal.*
Meh see-<u>en</u>-toh (mooy) mahl

579. I've been feeling sick since yesterday.
Me siento mal desde ayer.
Meh see-<u>en</u>-toh mahl <u>dess</u>-deh ah-<u>yehr</u>

since two days ago.   *desde hace dos días.*
<u>dess</u>-deh <u>ah</u>-seh dohss <u>dee</u>-ahss

since a week ago.   *desde hace una semana.*
<u>dess</u>-deh <u>ah</u>-seh <u>oo</u>-nah seh-<u>mah</u>-nah

since I got here.
desde que llegué.   <u>dess</u>-deh keh yeh-<u>geh</u>

580. I'm (very) sick.   *Estoy (muy) enfermo/-a.*
Ess-<u>toy</u> (mooy) en-<u>fehr</u>-moh/-ah

581. I need a doctor (who speaks English).
Necesito un médico/doctor (que hable inglés).
Neh-seh-<u>see</u>-toh oon <u>meh</u>-dee-koh/dohk-<u>tor</u> keh <u>ah</u>-bleh
een-<u>gless</u>

a general practitioner.   *un médico generalista.*
oon <u>meh</u>-dee-koh heh-nehr-ah-<u>lees</u>-tah

a specialist.   *un especialista.*   oon ess-peh-see-ahl-<u>ees</u>-tah

a dentist.   *un dentista.*   oon den-<u>tees</u>-tah

582. Where can I get a medical examination?
¿Dónde puedo obtener una consulta médica?
<u>Dohn</u>-deh <u>pweh</u>-doh ohb-teh-<u>nehr</u> <u>oo</u>-nah kohn-<u>sool</u>-tah
<u>meh</u>-dee-kah

583. I would rather see a female doctor.
Preferiría ver a una doctora.
Preh-feh-ree-<u>ree</u>-ah vehr ah <u>oo</u>-nah dohk-<u>tor</u>-ah

584. Can a doctor come here?   *¿Puede venir un doctor aquí?*
<u>Pweh</u>-deh ven-<u>eer</u> oon dohk-<u>tor</u> ah-<u>kee</u>

585. Call an ambulance.   *Llamen una ambulancia.*
<u>Yah</u>-men <u>oo</u>-nah ahm-boo-<u>lahn</u>-see-ah

586. I want to go to the hospital.   *Quiero ir al hospital.*
Kee-<u>eh</u>-roh eer ahl ohss-pee-<u>tahl</u>

to the clinic.   *a la clínica.*   ah lah <u>klee</u>-nee-kah

to the Emergency Room.
a la sala de emergencias/urgencias. (Mex.)
ah lah <u>sah</u>-lah deh eh-mehr-<u>hen</u>-see-ahss/oor-<u>hen</u>-see-ahss

587. Do I need to make an appointment?
¿Debo hacer una cita?
<u>Deh</u>-boh ah-<u>sehr</u> <u>oo</u>-nah <u>see</u>-tah

588. It's an emergency.   *Es una emergencia.*
Ess <u>oo</u>-nah eh-mehr-<u>hen</u>-see-ah

589. It's urgent.   *Es urgente.*   Ess oor-<u>hen</u>-teh

590. I have a (high) fever/a (high) temperature.
Tengo (mucha) fiebre/una temperatura (alta).
<u>Ten</u>-goh (<u>moo</u>-chah) fee-<u>eh</u>-breh/<u>oo</u>-nah tem-peh-rah-<u>too</u>-rah (<u>ahl</u>-tah)

591. I feel a (sharp) pain here.
Siento un (fuerte) dolor aquí.
See-<u>en</u>-toh oon (<u>fwehr</u>-teh) doh-<u>lor</u> ah-<u>kee</u>

592. [My head] hurts (a lot).   *Me duele (mucho) la cabeza.*
Meh <u>dweh</u>-leh (<u>moo</u>-choh) lah kah-<u>beh</u>-sah

My tooth . . .   . . . *el diente.*   el dee-<u>en</u>-teh

My neck . . .   . . . *el cuello.*   el <u>kweh</u>-yoh

My throat . . .   . . . *la garganta.*   lah gar-<u>gahn</u>-tah

My shoulder . . .   . . . *el hombro.*   el <u>ohm</u>-broh

My back . . .   . . . *la espalda.*   lah ess-<u>pahl</u>-dah

My chest . . .   . . . *el pecho.*   el <u>peh</u>-choh

My left/right arm . . .   . . . *el brazo izquierdo/derecho.*
el <u>brah</u>-soh ees-kee-<u>ehr</u>-doh/deh-<u>reh</u>-choh

My elbow . . .   . . . *el codo.*   el <u>koh</u>-doh

My wrist . . .   . . . *la muñeca.*   lah moo-<u>nyeh</u>-kah

My hand . . .   . . . *la mano.*   lah <u>mah</u>-noh

My finger . . .   . . . *el dedo.*   el <u>deh</u>-doh

My stomach . . .   . . . *el estomago.*   el ess-<u>toh</u>-mah-goh

My hip . . .   . . . *la cadera.*   lah kah-<u>deh</u>-rah

My leg . . .   . . . *la pierna.*   lah pee-<u>ehr</u>-nah

My knee . . .   . . . *la rodilla.*   lah roh-<u>dee</u>-yah

My foot . . .   . . . *el pie.*   el pee-<u>eh</u>

593. I'm dizzy.   *Estoy mareado/-a.*   Ess-<u>toy</u> mar-eh-<u>ah</u>-doh/-ah

constipated.   *constipado/-a/-estreñido/-a.*
kohn-stee-<u>pah</u>-doh/-ah/ess-treh-<u>nyee</u>-doh/-ah

bleeding (a lot).   *sangrando (mucho).*
sahn-<u>grahn</u>-doh (<u>moo</u>-choh)

594. It itches (a lot).   *Siento (mucha) comezón.*
See-<u>en</u>-toh (<u>moo</u>-chah) koh-<u>meh</u>-<u>sohn</u>

595. I feel nauseous.   *Siento náuseas.*   See-<u>en</u>-toh <u>now</u>-seh-ahss

596. I suffer from indigestion.   *Sufro de indigestión.*
<u>Soo</u>-froh deh een-dee-gess-tee-<u>ohn</u>

597. I suffer from heartburn.
Sufro de agruras/acidez estomacal.
<u>Soo</u>-froh deh ah-<u>groo</u>-rahss/ah-<u>see</u>-dess ess-toh-mah-<u>kahl</u>

598. I can't breathe.   *No puedo respirar.*
Noh <u>pweh</u>-doh ress-pee-<u>rar</u>

see (clearly).   *ver (claramente).*   vehr (klah-rah-<u>men</u>-teh)

hear (well).   *oír (bien).*   oh-<u>eer</u> (bee-<u>en</u>)

sleep.   *dormir.*   dor-<u>meer</u>

move my arm/my legs.   *mover el brazo/las piernas.*
moh-<u>vehr</u> el <u>brah</u>-soh/lahss pee-<u>ehr</u>-nahss

speak.   *hablar.*   ah-<u>blar</u>

599. Something I ate made me ill.   *Algo que comí me hizo daño.*
<u>Ahl</u>-goh keh koh-<u>mee</u> meh ee-soh <u>dah</u>-nyoh

600. I threw up (a lot).   *Vomité (mucho).*
Voh-mee-<u>teh</u> (<u>moo</u>-choh)

601. Something bit me. (an insect)   *Algo me picó.*
<u>Ahl</u>-goh meh pee-<u>koh</u>

602. Something bit me. (an animal)   *Algo me mordió.*
<u>Ahl</u>-goh meh mor-dee-<u>oh</u>

603. I hurt myself.   *Me lastimé.*   Meh lahss-tee-<u>meh</u>

604. I twisted my wrist/my ankle. *Me torcí la muñeca/el tobillo.*
Meh tor-<u>see</u> lah moo-<u>nyeh</u>-kah/el toh-<u>bee</u>-yoh

605. I broke my arm/my leg. *Me rompí el brazo/la pierna.*
Meh rohm-<u>pee</u> el <u>brah</u>-soh/lah pee-<u>ehr</u>-nah

606. I cut myself. *Me corté.* **Meh kor-<u>teh</u>**

607. I may need some stitches.
Puede que necesite unos puntos (de sutura).
<u>Pweh</u>-deh keh neh-seh-<u>see</u>-teh <u>oo</u>-nohss <u>poon</u>-tohss (deh soo-<u>too</u>-rah)

608. I burned myself. *Me quemé.* **Meh keh-<u>meh</u>**

609. I have asthma. *Tengo asma.* **<u>Ten</u>-goh <u>ahss</u>-mah**
muscle cramps. *calambres musculares.*
kah-<u>lahm</u>-bress moos-koo-<u>lah</u>-ress
cancer. *cáncer.* **<u>kahn</u>-sehr**
diabetes. *diabetes.* **dee-ah-<u>beh</u>-tess**
diarrhea. *diarrea.* **dee-ar-<u>reh</u>-ah**
menstrual cramps. *dolores menstruales.*
doh-<u>loh</u>-ress mens-<u>trwah</u>-less
chills. *escalofríos.* **ess-kah-loh-<u>free</u>-ohss**
an S.T.D. *una enfermedad venérea/sexual.*
<u>oo</u>-nah en-fehr-meh-<u>dahd</u> veh-<u>neh</u>-reh-ah/sek-soo-<u>ahl</u>
high/low blood pressure. *la presión alta/baja.*
lah preh-see-<u>ohn</u> <u>ahl</u>-tah/<u>bah</u>-hah
hepatitis. *hepatitis.* **eh-pah-<u>tee</u>-tees**
AIDS. *SIDA.* **<u>see</u>-dah**
a cough. *tos.* **tohss**

610. I think I have an ear infection.
Creo que tengo una infección del oído.
<u>Kreh</u>-oh keh <u>ten</u>-goh <u>oo</u>-nah een-fek-see-<u>ohn</u> del oh-<u>ee</u>-doh
a skin infection. *infección de la piel.*
een-fek-see-<u>ohn</u> deh lah pee-<u>el</u>
a urinary tract infection. *infección urinaria.*
een-fek-see-<u>ohn</u> oo-ree-<u>nah</u>-ree-ah

a yeast infection.   *infección vaginal.*
een-fek-see-<u>ohn</u> vah-hee-<u>nahl</u>

a bladder infection.   *infección de la vejiga.*
een-fek-see-<u>ohn</u> deh lah veh-<u>hee</u>-gah

611. I've had heart problems.   *He tenido problemas del corazón.*
Eh teh-<u>nee</u>-doh proh-<u>bleh</u>-mahss del koh-rah-<u>sohn</u>

liver problems.   *problemas del hígado.*
proh-<u>bleh</u>-mahss del <u>ee</u>-gah-doh

kidney problems.   *problemas renales.*
proh-<u>bleh</u>-mahss reh-<u>nah</u>-less

lung problems.   *problemas respiratorios.*
proh-<u>bleh</u>-mahss res-pee-rah-<u>toh</u>-ree-ohss

612. I'm allergic to penicillin.   *Soy alérgico a la penicilina.*
Soy ah-<u>lehr</u>-hee-koh ah lah peh-nee-see-<u>lee</u>-nah

to shellfish.   *a los mariscos.*   ah lohss mah-<u>rees</u>-kohss

to peanuts.   *a los cacahuates/al maní.*
ah lohss kah-kah-<u>wah</u>-tess/ahl mah-<u>nee</u>

to pollen.   *al polen.*   ahl <u>poh</u>-len

to bee stings.   *a las picaduras de abeja.*
ah lahss pee-kah-<u>doo</u>-rahss deh ah-<u>beh</u>-hah

613. I have hay fever.   *Tengo fiebre del heno.*
<u>Ten</u>-goh fee-<u>eh</u>-breh del <u>eh</u>-noh

614. My doctor prescribed this medicine.
Mi doctor me recetó esta medicina.
Mee dohk-<u>tor</u> meh reh-seh-<u>toh</u> <u>ess</u>-tah meh-dee-<u>see</u>-nah

615. I am taking pain-killers.   *Estoy tomando analgésicos.*
Ess-<u>toy</u> toh-<u>mahn</u>-doh ah-nahl-<u>heh</u>-see-kohss

antibiotics.   *antibióticos.*   ahn-tee-bee-<u>oh</u>-tee-kohss

antihistamines.   *antiestamínicos.*
ahn-tee-ess-tah-<u>mee</u>-nee-kohss

aspirin.   *aspirinas.*   ahss-pee-<u>ree</u>-nahss

contraceptive pills.
píldoras/pastillas anticonceptivas.
<u>peel</u>-doh-rahss/pahss-<u>tee</u>-yahss ahn-tee-kohn-sep-<u>tee</u>-vahss

vitamins.   *vitaminas.*   vee-tah-<u>mee</u>-nahss

616. I (don't) smoke.   *(No) Fumo.*   **(Noh) <u>Foo</u>-moh**

617. I (don't) drink alcohol.   *(No) Bebo alcohol.*
(Noh) <u>Beh</u>-boh ahl-<u>kohl</u>

618. I (don't) use drugs.   *(No) Uso drogas.*
(Noh) <u>Oo</u>-soh <u>droh</u>-gahss

619. I wear contact lenses.   *Uso lentes de contacto.*
<u>Oo</u>-soh <u>len</u>-tess deh kohn-<u>tahk</u>-toh

620. Is it (very) serious?   *¿Es (muy) grave?*
Ess (mooy) <u>grah</u>-veh

621. Will I be well (soon)?   *¿Estaré bien (pronto)?*
Ess-tah-<u>reh</u> bee-<u>en</u> (-<u>prohn</u>-toh)

622. How much for the visit?   *¿Cuánto es por la consulta?*
<u>Kwahn</u>-toh ess por lah kohn-<u>sool</u>-tah

623. I need a receipt for my insurance company.
Necesito un recibo para mi compañía de seguros.
Neh-seh-<u>see</u>-toh oon reh-<u>see</u>-boh <u>pah</u>-rah mee kohm-pah-<u>nyee</u>-ah deh seh-<u>goo</u>-rohss

624. Can you give me something for the pain? (for.)
¿Me puede dar algo para el dolor?
Meh <u>pweh</u>-deh dar <u>ahl</u>-goh <u>pah</u>-rah el doh-<u>lor</u>

625. I need medicine.   *Necesito medicina.*
Neh-seh-<u>see</u>-toh meh-dee-<u>see</u>-nah

    a Band-Aid.   *una curita/tirita. (Sp.)*
    <u>oo</u>-nah koo-<u>ree</u>-tah/tee-<u>ree</u>-tah

    a laxative.   *un laxante.*   **oon lahk-<u>sahn</u>-teh**

    a prescription.   *una receta médica.*
    <u>oo</u>-nah reh-<u>seh</u>-tah <u>meh</u>-dee-kah

    a tetanus shot.   *una vacuna contra el tétano.*
    <u>oo</u>-nah vah-<u>koo</u>-nah <u>kohn</u>-trah el <u>teh</u>-tah-noh

    a bandage.   *una venda.*   **<u>oo</u>-nah <u>ven</u>-dah**

626. I don't want to have surgery here.   *No quiero que me
operen aquí.*   **Noh kee-<u>eh</u>-roh keh meh oh-<u>peh</u>-ren ah-<u>kee</u>**

627. Where is the drugstore?   *¿Dónde está la farmacia?*
      Dohn-deh ess-**tah** lah far-**mah**-see-ah

628. Is it open twenty-four hours?
      ¿Está abierta las veinticuatro horas?
      Ess-**tah** ah-bee-**ehr**-tah lahss vayn-tee-**kwah**-troh **oh**-rahss

629. Are you a pharmacist? (for.)   *¿Es usted farmacéutico/-a?*
      Ess oos-**ted** fahr-mah-**seh**-oo-tee-koh/kah

630. How do you take this medicine?
      ¿Cómo se toma esta medicina?
      Koh-moh seh **toh**-mah **ess**-tah meh-dee-**see**-nah

631. Does this medicine cause side effects?
      ¿Causa efectos secundarios este medicamento?
      Kow-sah eh-**fek**-tohss seh-koon-**dah**-ree-ohss **ess**-teh
      meh-dee-kah-**men**-toh

CAR TROUBLE

632. The car broke down.
      Se descompuso el auto/el coche.
      Seh dess-kohm-**poo**-soh el **ow**-toh/el **koh**-cheh

633. We had an accident.   *Tuvimos un accidente.*
      Too-**vee**-mohss oon ahk-see-**den**-teh

634. We crashed (with another car).   *Chocamos (con otro auto).*
      Cho-**kah**-mohss (kohn **oh**-troh **ow**-toh)

635. It won't start.   *No enciende.*   Noh en-see-**en**-deh

636. It makes a funny noise.   *Hace un ruido raro.*
      Ah-seh oon **rwee**-doh **rah**-roh

637. It doesn't shift gears (smoothly).   *No embraga (fácilmente).*
      Noh em-**brah**-gah (**fah**-seel-men-teh)

638. It accelerates by itself.   *Acelera sólo.*
      Ah-ceh-**leh**-rah **soh**-loh

639.   The pedal gets stuck.   *El pedal se atora.*
       El peh-<u>dahl</u> seh ah-<u>toh</u>-rah

640.   The steering doesn't work.   *No funciona la dirección.*
       Noh foon-see-<u>oh</u>-nah lah dee-rek-see-<u>ohn</u>

641.   It's blowing a lot of smoke.
       Echa mucho humo.
       <u>Eh</u>-chah <u>moo</u>-choh <u>oo</u>-moh

642.   It has a flat tire.   *Tiene una rueda pinchada.*
       Tee-<u>eh</u>-neh <u>oo</u>-nah <u>rweh</u>-dah peen-<u>chah</u>-dah

643.   A tire went flat.   *Se le ponchó una llanta. (Mex.)*
       <u>Seh</u> leh pohn-<u>choh</u> <u>oo</u>-nah <u>yahn</u>-tah

644.   I think it has a dead battery.
       Creo que tiene la batería descargada.
       <u>Kreh</u>-oh keh tee-<u>eh</u>-neh lah bah-teh-<u>ree</u>-ah dess-kar-<u>gah</u>-dah

645.   It's overheated.   *Está sobrecalentado.*
       Ess-<u>tah</u> <u>soh</u>-breh-kah-len-<u>tah</u>-doh

646.   It's leaking coolant.   *Está perdiendo anticongelante.*
       Ess-<u>tah</u> pehr-dee-<u>en</u>-doh ahn-tee-kohn-heh-<u>lahn</u>-teh

647.   It needs oil.   *Le falta aceite.*   Leh <u>fahl</u>-tah ah-<u>say</u>-teh
       gas.   *gasolina.*   gahss-soh-<u>lee</u>-nah
       air in the tires.   *aire a las llantas.*   <u>I</u>-reh ah lahss <u>yahn</u>-tahss

648.   I left the keys inside.   *Dejé las llaves adentro.*
       Deh-<u>heh</u> lahss <u>yah</u>-vess ah-<u>den</u>-troh

649.   Where is there a car repair shop/garage?
       ¿Dónde hay un taller mecánico/un garaje?
       <u>Dohn</u>-deh I oon tah-<u>yehr</u> meh-<u>kah</u>-nee-koh/oon gah-<u>rah</u>-heh

650.   I need a tow truck.   *Necesito una grúa.*
       Neh-seh-<u>see</u>-toh <u>oo</u>-nah <u>groo</u>-ah

651.   Do you have jumper cables?
       ¿Tiene cables/una pinza de batería? (Sp.)
       Tee-<u>eh</u>-neh <u>kah</u>-bless/<u>oo</u>-nah <u>peen</u>-sah deh bah-teh-<u>ree</u>-ah

652. How much will it cost?   *¿Cuánto va a costar?*
      Kwahn-toh vah ah kohs-tar

653. Does that include parts and labor?
      ¿Eso incluye mano de obra y refacciones?
      Eh-soh een-kloo-yeh mah-noh deh oh-brah ee
      reh-fahk-see-oh-ness

654. Will you put in new parts? (for.)
      ¿Le pondrá refacciones nuevas?
      Leh pohn-drah reh-fahk-see-oh-ness nweh-vahss

655. Can you fix it (today)? (for.)
      ¿Puede arreglarlo/repararlo (hoy mismo)?
      Pweh-deh ah-reh-glar-loh/re-pah-rar-loh (oy mees-moh)

656. When will it be ready?   *¿Cuándo estará listo?*
      Kwahn-doh ess-tah-rah lees-toh

657. At what time can I pick it up?
      ¿A qué hora puedo recogerlo?
      Ah keh oh-rah pweh-doh reh-koh-hehr-loh

658. It's (not) insured.   *(No) Está asegurado.*
      (Noh) Ess-tah ah-seh-goo-rah-doh

659. Can I pay with a credit card?
      ¿Puedo pagar con tarjeta de crédito?
      Pweh-doh pah-gar kohn tar-heh-tah deh kreh-dee-toh

EMERGENCIES

660. Help!   *¡Ayuda!/¡Auxilio!/¡Socorro!*
      Ah-yoo-dah/Owk-see-lee-oh/Soh-koh-roh

661. Do you know first aid?   *¿Sabe primeros auxilios?*
      Sah-beh pree-meh-rohss owk-see-lee-ohss

662. I need a doctor.   *Necesito un médico/un doctor.*
      Neh-seh-see-toh oon meh-dee-koh/oon dohk-tor

663. Where is the nearest hospital?
      ¿Dónde está el hospital más cercano?
      Dohn-deh ess-tah el ohss-pee-tahl mahss sehr-kah-noh

664. Take me to the Emergency Room.
Lléveme a la sala de emergencias/urgencias. (Mex.)
<u>Yeh</u>-veh-meh ah lah <u>sah</u>-lah deh eh-mehr-<u>hen</u>-see-ahss/
oor-<u>hen</u>-see-ahss

665. I'm going to pass out.   *Me voy a desmayar.*
Meh voy ah dess-mah-<u>yahr</u>

666. Call the police. (pl.)   *Llamen a la policía.*
<u>Yah</u>-men ah lah poh-lee-<u>see</u>-ah

an ambulance.   *una ambulancia.*
<u>oo</u>-nah ahm-boo-<u>lahn</u>-see-ah

the fire department.   *a los bomberos.*
ah lohss bohm-<u>beh</u>-rohss

667. It's an emergency!   *¡Es una emergencia!*
Ess <u>oo</u>-nah eh-mehr-<u>hen</u>-see-ah

668. Do something, please. (for.)   *Haga algo, por favor.*
<u>Ah</u>-gah <u>ahl</u>-goh por fah-<u>vor</u>

669. Stop, thief!   *¡Alto, ladrón!*   <u>Ahl</u>-toh, lah-<u>drohn</u>

670. He went that way.   *Se fue por allá.*   Seh fweh por ah-<u>yah</u>

671. I have been robbed/assaulted.   *Me han robado/asaltado.*
Meh ahn roh-<u>bah</u>-doh/ah-sahl-<u>tah</u>-doh

672. They stole my wallet.   *Me robaron la cartera/la billetera.*
Meh roh-<u>bah</u>-ron lah kar-<u>teh</u>-rah/lah bee-yeh-<u>teh</u>-rah

673. They took my purse.
Se llevaron mi bolsa (Mex.)/mi bolso. (Sp.)
Seh yeh-<u>vah</u>-rohn mee <u>bohl</u>-sah/mee <u>bohl</u>-soh

my luggage.   *mi equipaje.*   mee eh-kee-<u>pah</u>-heh

674. I was raped.   *Me violaron.*   Meh vee-oh-<u>lah</u>-ron

675. I need to report a crime.   *Necesito hacer una denuncia.*
Neh-seh-<u>see</u>-toh ah-<u>sehr</u> <u>oo</u>-nah deh-<u>noon</u>-see-ah

676. I lost my passport.   *Perdí mi pasaporte.*
Pehr-<u>dee</u> mee pah-sah-<u>por</u>-teh

my money.   *mi dinero.*   mee dee-<u>neh</u>-roh

my ticket.   *mi boleto/pasaje.*   mee boh-<u>leh</u>-toh/pah-<u>sah</u>-heh

677. I can't find the key to my room.
     No encuentro la llave de mi habitación.
     Noh en-<u>kwen</u>-troh lah <u>yah</u>-veh deh mee ah-bee-tah-see-<u>ohn</u>

FAMILY, CHILDREN & PETS

678. I brought my family.   *Traje a mi familia.*
     <u>Trah</u>-heh ah mee fah-<u>meel</u>-yah

     my parents.   *a mis padres.*   **ah mees <u>pah</u>-dress**
     my in-laws.   *a mis suegros.*   **ah mees <u>sweh</u>-grohss**

679. I'm here with my (favorite) aunt and uncle.
     Estoy aquí con mis tíos (favoritos).
     Ess-<u>toy</u> ah-<u>kee</u> kohn mees <u>tee</u>-ohss (fah-voh-<u>ree</u>-tohss)

680. How many brothers/sisters do you have?
     ¿Cuántos hermanos/as tienes?
     <u>Kwahn</u>-tohss ehr-<u>mah</u>-nohss/ahss tee-<u>eh</u>-ness

681. I have one brother and one sister.
     Tengo un hermano y una hermana.
     <u>Ten</u>-goh oon ehr-<u>mah</u>-noh ee <u>oo</u>-nah ehr-<u>mah</u>-nah

682. These are my children.   *Estos son mis hijos/as.*
     <u>Ess</u>-tohss sohn mees <u>ee</u>-hohss/ahss

683. How old are your children? (for./inf.)
     ¿Cuántos años tienen sus/tus hijos/as?
     <u>Kwahn</u>-tohss <u>ah</u>-nyohss tee-<u>eh</u>-nen soos/toos <u>ee</u>-hohss/ahss

684. They are three and five years old.   *Tienen tres y cinco años.*
     Tee-<u>eh</u>-nen trehss ee <u>seen</u>-koh <u>ah</u>-nyohss

685. Where's your mom/dad?   *¿Dónde está tu mamá/papá?*
     <u>Dohn</u>-deh ess-<u>tah</u> too mah-<u>mah</u>/pah-<u>pah</u>

686. Are there children's activities?   *¿Hay actividades para niños?*
     I ahk-tee-vee-<u>dah</u>-dess <u>pah</u>-rah <u>nee</u>-nyohss

687. Where can we find a playground?
     ¿Dónde podemos encontrar un lugar de juegos/recreo?
     <u>Dohn</u>-deh poh-<u>deh</u>-mohss en-kohn-<u>trar</u> oon loo-<u>gar</u> de <u>hweh</u>-gohss/reh-<u>kreh</u>-oh

an amusement park?   *un parque de atracciones?*
oon <u>par</u>-keh deh ah-trahk-see-<u>oh</u>-ness

a children's museum?   *un museo para niños?*
oon moo-<u>seh</u>-oh <u>pah</u>-rah <u>nee</u>-nyohss

688. We're looking for a park with swings.
Estamos buscando un parque con columpios.
Ess-<u>tah</u>-mohss boos-<u>kahn</u>-doh oon <u>par</u>-keh kohn
koh-<u>loom</u>-pee-ohss

689. Do you know of a children's show? (for.)
¿Sabe de un espectáculo para niños?
<u>Sah</u>-beh deh oon ess-pek-<u>tah</u>-koo-loh <u>pah</u>-rah <u>nee</u>-nyohss

690. Isn't there a kiddy pool somewhere?
¿No hay una alberca para niños en algún lado?
Noh I <u>oo</u>-nah ahl-<u>behr</u>-kah <u>pah</u>-rah <u>nee</u>-nyohss en ahl-<u>goon</u>
<u>lah</u>—doh

691. Where can we find a toy store?
¿Dónde podemos encontrar una juguetería?
<u>Dohn</u>-deh poh-<u>deh</u>-mohss en-kohn-<u>trar</u> <u>oo</u>-nah
hoo-geh-teh-<u>ree</u>-ah

692. Do you sell educational games?   *¿Venden juegos educativos?*
<u>Ven</u>-den <u>hweh</u>-gohss eh-doo-kah-<u>tee</u>-vohss

693. Do you have children's books?   *¿Tienen libros para niños?*
Tee-<u>eh</u>-nen <u>lee</u>-brohss <u>pah</u>-rah <u>nee</u>-nyohss

694. Can we go in the museum with the stroller?
¿Podemos entrar al museo con el cochecito/la carriola? (Mex.)
Poh-<u>deh</u>-mohss en-<u>trar</u> ahl moo-<u>seh</u>-oh kohn el koh-cheh-<u>see</u>-
toh/lah kah-ree-<u>oh</u>-lah

695. We prefer a family-friendly restaurant.
Preferimos un restaurante para familias.
Preh-feh-<u>ree</u>-mohss oon res-tow-<u>rahn</u>-teh <u>pah</u>-rah
fah-<u>meel</u>-yahss

696. Do you have a children's menu?
¿Tienen un menú para niños?
Tee-<u>eh</u>-nen oon meh-<u>noo</u> <u>pah</u>-rah <u>nee</u>-nyohss

697. Can you bring us a high chair? (for.)
      ¿Nos puede traer una silla alta?
      Nohss <u>pweh</u>-deh trah-<u>ehr</u> <u>oo</u>-nah <u>see</u>-yah <u>ahl</u>-tah

698. We need to see a pediatrician.
      Necesitamos ver a un pediatra.
      Neh-seh-see-<u>tah</u>-mohss vehr ah oon peh-dee-<u>ah</u>-trah

699. Can we have pets in the room?
      ¿Podemos tener mascotas en la habitación?
      **Poh-<u>deh</u>-mohss teh-<u>nehr</u> mahss-<u>koh</u>-tahss en lah
      ah-bee-tah-see-<u>ohn</u>**

700. I'm going to walk the dog.
      Voy a pasear al perro.
      Voy ah pah-seh-<u>ar</u> ahl <u>peh</u>-roh

701. Where do they sell animal food?
      ¿Dónde se vende comida para animales?
      <u>Dohn</u>-deh seh <u>ven</u>-deh koh-<u>mee</u>-dah <u>pah</u>-rah ah-nee-<u>mah</u>-less

702. We have to take him/her to the vet.
      Tenemos que llevarlo/la al veterinario.
      Teh-<u>neh</u>-mohss keh yeh-<u>var</u>-loh/lah ahl veh-teh-ree-<u>nah</u>-ree-oh

703. Where is the animal hospital?
      ¿Dónde está el hospital para animales?
      <u>Dohn</u>-deh ess-<u>tah</u> el ohss-pee-<u>tahl</u> <u>pah</u>-rah ah-nee-<u>mah</u>-less

704. He/she is housebroken/trained.
      Está entrenado/a.
      Ess-<u>tah</u> en-treh-<u>nah</u>-doh/ah

705. He/she has all her vaccines.
      Tiene todas sus vacunas.
      Tee-<u>eh</u>-neh <u>toh</u>-dahss soos vah-<u>koo</u>-nahss

Spanish Grammar Primer

This section offers some vocabulary tips and the barest essentials of Spanish grammar. It is a helpful resource for a beginner and can serve as a quick reference for a more advanced speaker.

Abstract grammar can be very helpful, but the best way to integrate language rules will always be through frequent real-life use. Listen to as much Spanish as you can (music, movies, and television are good resources), communicate in Spanish as often as you can, using the words and phrases in this book, and soon you won't need to think about the grammar at all.

English and Spanish Cognates

Cognates are words that derive from a common ancestor language. Most words in Spanish and many words in English come from Latin or Greek. As a result, there are a lot of words in English that are cognates of words in Spanish; most are easily recognizable. Since changes are slight and predictable, you can quickly expand your vocabulary in Spanish by taking note of the following:

1. Some words are the same in both languages (except that their pronunciation may vary, see below): color, crisis, drama, error, general, horror, probable, tropical, . . .
2. Some words add an extra vowel to the English word: cliente, evidente, ignorante, importante, parte, artista, pianista, problema, programa, contacto, perfecto, líquido, . . .*

---

* Please don't make the error, often parodied in movies, of thinking that adding an "o" at the end of every word in a sentence makes it sound like Spanish; native Spanish speakers will likely consider it rude.

3. Many words ending in ty in English end in **tad** or **dad** in Spanish: facul**tad**, liber**tad**, curiosi**dad**, socie**dad**, eterni**dad**, capaci**dad**, reali**dad**, clari**dad**, . . .

4. Many words ending in y in English end in **ía**, **ia**, or **io** (depending on gender, see below): compañ**ía**, geograf**ía**, histor**ia**, farmac**ia**, diccionar**io**, ordinar**io**, . . .*

5. Words that end in tion in English generally end in **ción** in Spanish: na**ción**, administra**ción**, ac**ción**, fric**ción**, sec**ción**, emo**ción**, combina**ción**, contribu**ción**, . . .

6. Words that end in ous in English often end in **oso** in Spanish: gen**eroso**, fam**oso**, preci**oso**, delici**oso**, tedi**oso**, contagi**oso**, curi**oso**, escandal**oso**, religi**oso**, . . .

Gender, Number, and Agreement

In Spanish, most nouns are gendered: *silla* (chair) and *mesa* (table) are feminine while *escritorio* (desk) and *sombrero* (hat) are masculine. However, not all feminine nouns end in **a**, nor do all masculine nouns end in **o**: *carne* (meat), *flor* (flower), *canción* (song), and *mano* (hand) are feminine, while *sobre* (envelope), *calor* (heat), *camión* (bus), and *clima* (weather) are masculine. In some cases, the gender of a noun will depend on the object to which it applies: *cantante* (singer) can be either feminine or masculine. Likewise, *orden* (order) is feminine when it refers to the order issued by an authority and masculine when it refers to the order of things.

The best way to figure out whether a noun is masculine or feminine is to look at its corresponding definite (*the*) or indefinite (*a/an/some*) article:

	Definite (*the*)		Indefinite (*a/an/some*)	
	Masculine	Feminine	Masculine	Feminine
Singular	el	la	un	una
Plural	los	las	unos	unas

It is important to be aware of noun gender because in Spanish, articles and adjectives belonging to a noun must agree in gender with the noun.

---

* In a few cases, cognates don't have exactly the same meaning in Spanish as they do in English: *policía* means "police" in Spanish; policy should be translated as *política*.

Esa flor azul es muy bonita.*	*That blue flower is very pretty.*
María es **una** cantante muy talentosa.	*María is a very talented singer.*
Pedro es **un** cantante muy talentoso.	*Pedro is a very talented singer.*

Likewise, nouns, adjectives, and articles must agree in number. In Spanish, plurality is expressed by adding an **s** to words that end in a vowel, and **es** to nouns that end in a consonant:

Las flores azules son mis preferidas.	*Blue flowers are my favorite.*
Pedro y **María** son **unos** cantantes muy buenos.†	*Pedro and María are very good singers.*

Possessive Adjectives

In Spanish possession is generally indicated by a set of adjectives which must agree in gender and number with the noun they describe, the possessed object.

my	mi/mis
your	tu/tus
your (for.)	su/sus
his	
her	
our	nuestro/nuestra/nuestros/nuestras
your (pl.)	vuestro/vuestra/vuestros/vuestras (Sp.)
	su/sus (L. Am.)
their	su/sus

---

* Adjectives that end in e or a consonant don't change on account of gender:
La casa verde   *The green house*   El sombrero verde   *The green hat*
† When there are both feminine and masculine individuals or objects in a group, masculine adjectives and articles are used.

Mi casa es su casa.	*My house is your house. (for).* *
Su pelo es rubio y sus ojos son verdes.	*His/her hair is blond and his/her eyes are green.* †
Tenemos **nuestro** dinero y nuestras maletas.‡	We have our money and our suitcases.
Pedro y Juan están listos para su viaje.	*Pedro and Juan are ready for their trip.*

Diminutives

Diminutives are widely used in Spanish, particularly in Latin American Spanish. A diminutive can signify that something is smaller, but it can also serve to express endearment, to intensify an idea, or as a rhetorical device that "softens" and embellishes whatever is being said. Diminutives are particles that attach at the end of words either after the final consonant or by replacing the final vowel. There are a number of diminutive suffixes in Spanish, but the most common is **ito(s)/-ita(s)**.

Sólo quiero un pedac**ito** muy pequeñ**ito** de pastel.
I only want a tiny little piece of cake.

Me llamo Juan, pero mis amigos me llaman Juan**ito**.
My name is John, but my friends call me Johnny.

Vivo en una cas**ita** muy linda con mis hij**itas** y mis perr**itos**.
I live in a very cute little house with my dear little daughters and my doggies.

---

* On formal address see the PRONOUNS section on p. 75.

† In Spanish the gender of the possessor is not expressed by the possessive adjective. Gender information would be supplied by context or through an alternative structure such as: El pelo de María es rubio y **sus** ojos son verdes (*María's hair is blond and her eyes are green*).

‡ Of all the possessive adjectives, only the first person plural (nuestros/as) and the second person plural (vuestros/as) that is used in Spain (See PRONOUNS section beginning on p. 75) express gender by switching between "o" and "a" at the end.

Pronouns

Pronouns in Spanish function mostly as they do in English; they are used to replace the subject or the objects in a sentence to improve speech flow. Since they are an essential part of everyday speech, it is important to know a few things about personal pronouns in Spanish.

Subject[1]		Indirect Object		Direct Object		Reflexive Object[5]	
yo	*I*	me	*to me*	me	*me*	me	*myself*
tú	*you*	te	*to you*	te	*you*	te	*yourself*
usted[2]	*you (formal)*	le [se][4]	*to you, to him/ her, to it*	lo, la	*you (formal)*	se	*yourself, him/ herself, itself*[6]
él	*he*			lo	*him, it m.*		
ella	*she*			la	*her, it f.*		
nosotros/ as	*we*	nos	*to us*	nos	*us*	nos	*ourselves*
voso- tros/as[3]	*you pl.*	os	*to you pl.*	os	*you pl.*	os	*your- selves*
ustedes	*you pl.*	les [se]	*to you, to them*	los, las	*you pl.*	se	*your- selves, them- selves*
ellos	*they m.*			los	*them m.*		*them- selves*
ellas	*they f.*			las	*them f.*		

TABLE NOTE 1. In Spanish a verb's conjugation generally corresponds to a specific subject, therefore subject pronouns can be, and often are, omitted. Note that Spanish does not have an equivalent of the subject pronoun "it:"

Está lloviendo.   *It is raining.*   ¿Quién era?   *Who was it?*

TABLE NOTE 2. ***Usted*** *(Ud.)* is a more formal way of addressing a second person; it is used to address people of a superior rank (elders, bosses, officials, etc.) and with new acquaintances. Formal address uses the verb forms and pronouns of the third person as a way of setting a respectful distance between speaker and addressee. Compare the following sentences:

Formal: ¿Cómo **está** (usted)?   *How are you?*
No quiero molestar**lo**.   *I don't want to bother you.*

Informal: ¿Cómo **estás** (tú)?   *How are you?*
No quiero molestar**te**.   *I don't want to bother you.*

Usted is used systematically in Latin America where it is considered polite, but only sporadically in Spain.

TABLE NOTE 3. **Vosotros/as** and **Ustedes** are used to address a group (some English dialects use "you all" or "y'all" for the same purpose). **Vosotros/as** has its own set of verb forms and pronouns, while **ustedes** uses those of the third person plural. Although **ustedes** is the plural form of **usted**, no formality is necessarily implied. **Vosotros/as** is only used in Spain.

TABLE NOTE 4. Object pronouns can precede an active verb or be attached at the end of an infinitive, a gerund, or an affirmative command:

Quiero comer una manzana. >   **La** quiero comer. = Quiero comer**la**.

I want to eat an apple. >   *I want to eat it.*

Estoy comiendo una manzana. >   **La** estoy comiendo. = Estoy comiéndo**la**.

I am eating an apple. >   *I am eating it.*

¡Come la manzana! > ¡Cóme**la**!   but   ¡No comas la manzana! > ¡No **la** comas!

Eat the apple. >   *Eat it.*   *Don't eat the apple.* > *Don't eat it.*

Direct objects can appear in a sentence as either a noun or a pronoun but not both. However, indirect object pronouns <u>must be used</u> whether or not the indirect object noun appears in the sentence:

Pedro **me** da dinero (**a mí**).   *Pedro gives money to me.*
Juan **le** da flores (**a María**).   *Juan gives flowers to María.*

When using two object pronouns, the indirect object pronoun <u>always</u> comes first:

Pedro **me lo** da.   *Pedro gives it to me.*

When combined with the direct object pronouns **lo**, **la**, **los**, or **las**, the indirect object pronoun **le** changes to **se**:

Juan **se las** da (**a María**).   *Juan gives **them to her** (to María).*

TABLE NOTE 5. As in English, **reflexive pronouns** are used to "reflect" or return the action expressed by the verb back upon the subject:

Me veo en el espejo.	*I see myself in the mirror.*
María **se** viste.	*María dresses (herself).*

Common reflexive actions include getting up (*levantarse*), washing (*lavarse*) or bathing (*bañarse*), sitting (*sentarse*), lying down (*acostarse*), and falling asleep (*dormirse*). However, as long as it makes sense, any verb can be made to describe a reflexive action by adding a reflexive pronoun. Sometimes reflexivity is added for emphasis or precision. Compare the following:

romper *to break*	Rompiste la ventana.	*You broke the window.*
romper**se** *to break*	**Te** rompiste la pierna.	*You broke **your** leg.*
dormir *to sleep*	Juan está durmiendo.	*Juan is sleeping.*
dormir**se** *to fall asleep*	Juan está durmiéndo**se**.	*Juan is falling asleep.*
ir *to go*	Vamos al cine.	*Let's go to the movies.*
ir**se** *to leave, to go away*	Vámo**nos** al cine.	*Let's leave for the movies.*

Note that reflexive pronouns follow similar positioning rules as object pronouns.

TABLE NOTE 6. In Spanish the pronoun **se** is very often used to express a passive or an impersonal action in which the object may assume the function of the subject (which creates a reflexive-like expression):

En México **se** habla español.	*Spanish is spoken in Mexico. / People speak Spanish in Mexico.*
No **se** debe desperdiciar agua.	*Water mustn't be wasted. / One mustn't waste water.*

Negativity

In a negative sentence, a negative word <u>must</u> come before the verb and any preceding pronouns:

No te quiero pero **nunca** te lo había dicho.	*I do not love you but I had never told you.*

Spanish actually requires double, and even triple negatives. Negativity must be expressed throughout the sentence:

Nunca has querido a **nadie**.	*You have never loved anyone.*
Nadie quiere ir **nunca** a **ningún** lado conmigo.	*No one ever wants to go anywhere with me.*

Verbs, Tenses, and Moods

Ser vs. Estar

English translates both the verb *ser* and the verb *estar* as "to be." However, in Spanish they have very different meanings. *Ser* is used to talk about essences (aspects that are perceived as being inherent to or definitive of the subject) and about time. *Estar* is used to talk about states (aspects or conditions that are merely circumstantial to the subject) and about location (space). Compare the following sentences:

Pedro **es** un tipo simpático pero hoy **está** enojado.	*Pedro is a nice guy but today he is angry.*
Son las dos y María todavía **está** dormida.*	*It is two o'clock and María is still asleep.*
La casa que **está** en esa colina **es** amarilla.	*The house that is on that hill is yellow.*
La fiesta **fue** en la casa que **está** en venta.†	*The party was at the house that is for sale.*

The verb *estar* is used in combination with a gerund to form progressive tenses:

Estoy escribiendo en la computadora.	*I am writing on the computer.*
Estábamos pensando en llamarte.	*We were thinking about calling you.*

Verbs like <u>gustar</u>

The verb *gustar* is generally, and accurately, translated as "to like":

A Juan **le gustan** los postres.	*Juan likes desserts.*

In Spanish, however, Juan is not the subject of the verb *gustan* but its indirect object, while *los postres* functions as both subject and direct

---

* States can be permanent. In Spanish, death is considered a state: Las plantas de mi casa **están** muertas (*My house plants are dead*).

† Since events involve a lot more than their location, the verb **ser** is used to talk about parties and ceremonies in general: la boda **será** en la catedral (*The wedding will be in the cathedral*).

object. Note that the verb agrees with *los postres* and that *le* agrees with Juan. Therefore, a more literal translation would be: "Desserts are pleasing to Juan." There are a number of verbs that function like *gustar*. Consider the following examples:

María **le gusta** a Pedro.* *Pedro likes María. (lit. María is pleasing to Pedro.)*

(A Ana y a Luis) No **les interesa** la ciencia.† *Science doesn't interest them (Ana and Luis).*

(A mí) **Me preocupa** llegar tarde a mi cita. *Being late for my appointment worries me.*

Other common verbs that function like *gustar* include *encantar* (to really like), *importar* (to matter), *aburrir* (to bore), *quedar* (to have left), *faltar* (to lack), and *doler* (to hurt). It is interesting to note that this type of verb generally expresses subjective perceptions and is used to talk about things the subject finds pleasing, boring, important, or painful.

Preterit vs. Imperfect

The preterit tense is used when a past action is considered singular and definitely concluded:

Pasé un mes en Madrid el año pasado. *I spent a month in Madrid last year.*

Fue entonces cuando **conocí** a Juan. *It was then that I met Juan.*

The imperfect tense is used for recurring actions in the past or actions which happened over an indefinite period of time in the past:

Antes, **iba** a Madrid cada año. *Before, I used to go to Madrid every year.*

En esa época, Juan **estudiaba** leyes. *At the time, Juan studied (was studying) law.*

---

* In Spanish object nouns can precede the verb; the preposition "a" is used to avoid confusion when two possible agents are involved (i.e., Mary might be the one who likes Pedro).
† The indirect-object pronoun is necessary, but the indirect object itself may be omitted or included to add precision to the sentence.

The preterit and the imperfect are often combined in a sentence to emphasize certain actions (preterit) over others that provide context or serve as backdrop (imperfect):

Decidí comer mientras te **esperaba.**   *I decided to eat lunch while I waited (was waiting) for you.*

Llovía cuando **llegó** el avión.   *It was raining when the plane arrived.*

Subjunctive mood

In Spanish, the subjunctive mood is used to express possibility, uncertainty, and empathy. When speaking about actions that happen in the present, happened in the past, or will happen in the future, the indicative mood is used. For talking about actions which may (or may not) happen, or may (or may not) have happened, the subjunctive mood is used. In general, the subjunctive is used to talk about situations that are beyond the control of a sentence's primary subject. For instance, we may say that it is important, necessary even, for drivers to come to a full stop at a stop sign which, however, does not guarantee that they will. Likewise, even if Juan wanted Pedro to lend him money, Pedro might have refused. Finally, a person may feel sorry about another's tragedy, but be unable to do anything to change it. Consider the following examples:

Es posible que **vaya** a México en verano.*
It is possible that I will go to Mexico in the summer.

Es importante (necesario) que los conductores **respeten** las señales de tránsito.
It is important (necessary) that drivers respect traffic signals.

Juan quería que Pedro le **prestara** dinero.†
Juan wanted Pedro to lend him money.

---

* A subjunctive clause depends, at least implicitly, on an indicative statement; they are linked by a conjunctive element, most often "que." In other words, possibility must always be grounded in reality.

† Generally, if the verb in the main clause is in the present tense, the verb in the subjunctive clause will also be in the present. Likewise, a past-tense verb in the main clause calls for the past tense in the subjunctive clause.

Siento que **hayas perdido** tu vuelo.
I am sorry that you (have) missed your flight.

In Spanish *pensar* (to think) and *creer* (to believe) express certainty on the part of the primary subject. Therefore, the subjunctive is unnecessary. However, lack of belief does not rule out possibility altogether; therefore the subjunctive is appropriate. Compare the following sentences:

María **cree** (**piensa**) que existen los fantasmas, pero yo **no pienso** (**creo**) que existan.

María believes (thinks) ghosts exist, but I don't think (believe) that they do.

When a single subject is involved in the action there is no need to introduce a subjunctive clause; the verb in the infinitive is used in the main clause instead. Compare the following sentences:

Quiero que (tú) **aprendas** español.   *I want you to learn Spanish*

Quiero **aprender** español.   *I want to learn Spanish.*

Index